~~One One Coco~~

*The Modern Day Guide to
Long Distance Relationships*

~~One One Coco~~

The Modern Day Guide to Long Distance Relationships

How to Build, Maintain, and Grow Your
Long Distance Relationship

HARONA OSBORNE

G
GORDON HOUSE PRESS

ISBN-10: 069217768X
ISBN-13: 978-0692177686

– DEDICATION –

This book is for everyone who finds themselves in love from a distance. A long-distance relationship has many descriptions but my favorite word to use to describe it is hope. I dedicate this book to all long-distance lovers who believe in faith and hope.

CONTENTS

"ONE ONE COCO FULL BASKET"

This expression comes from the island of Jamaica, where I was born and raised. One One Coco Full Basket refers to the idea that we must take a process one step at a time, to achieve the outcomes that we desire. As you read this book, I want you to carry this principle into your spirit. Using the tools that I share in this book, practice how to take things one step at a time in your relationship. Approaching your long-distance relationship one step at a time is the most efficient, and most fulfilling way to get to your goal. There are many difficulties in a long-distance relationship, but there is also an abundance of happiness and hope. Choose to believe in joy and hope. Approach your relationship one step at a time, one day at a time. Likewise, always remember that One One Coco Full Basket.

1

– INTRODUCTION –

Statistics show that there are over 14 million people in the United States today who consider themselves as being in a long-distance relationship, yet there is a lack in current and urbane literature to help us navigate this incredibly unique relationship structure. There are a few long-distance lovers, like me, with the tools needed to keep and grow a long-distance relationship; however, there has not been any modern-day representation for our community, until now.

I have been a long-distance girlfriend, a long-distance friend with benefits, long distance fiancé (twice), and married long distance. I have also been long distance deceived, and long distance with no conceivable way of being together. I have seen it all. I have dated long distance my entire adult life, and so I am fully aware, and fully equipped with the tools that are necessary to build, support, and to grow a long-distance relationship. I share some of these tools with you in this book.

I have not given much thought to why my choice has been to date long distance, but I do believe that there is a higher purpose for all of us in this world, and I do not encourage limiting ourselves to our immediate environment. One of my favorite quotes is, "if you are going to own something, own experience." I am not sure who initially said this quote, but I fell in love with it because it expressively captures the essence of long-distance dating.

I am a strong advocate for an experience. We must go out into the world and explore. Love, lose and regain. Experience what it means to live an abundant, and free life. When I look back fifty years from now, I want to be able to say that I had done all the things that many before me, and many after me, did not dare to do. I will know that I lived my best life, with no apologies. People will call me brave because I decided to take chances. I have experienced distinct kinds of love, with different understandings, misunderstandings, and outcomes. I have mastered the good and the evil. I will be able to say fifty years from today, that I own experience.

Being in a long-distance relationship is a time in your life when you decide to take a chance. Look at yourself in the mirror and remind yourself that you have made a bold choice. You are brave for making a decision that most people would not even consider. Even with free will, many still would not dream of taking this chance on love.

Long distance relationships often lead to many misunderstandings. The point of a long-distance relationship is to bring lovers together. It is not meant to divide love or to separate you from the one you love. That is just the unfortunate state of the relationship. The purpose of a long-distance relationship is to connect two people who love each other, from where ever they are in the world. Regardless of how you ended up in a long-distance relationship, the significance of the relationship is that it is meant to keep you connected with your partner.

A long-distance relationship is a transition tool that you and your partner will use to get you to a mutual physical space, in the shortest period. This period differs for every couple. Some long-distance couples stay separated for months before they come together in one physical area, while others take many years to get to that point. Every long-distance couple will have their journey and their timeline. The most important thing is that you are consistently, and actively working to get to this point. Your relationship must lead to an end where you are both physically together. There must be effective planning for this to happen sometime in the future; otherwise, you are wasting your time and mental energy.

Always remember that the point of a long-distance relationship is to bring together, not to keep apart. There must be an "end goal" in the relationship. The end goal of a long-distance relationship should be the same for every couple. The end goal refers to the intent of being together physically in one place or living together in the same space. This place can be marriage, or just simply living together under the same roof.

The end goal of the relationship becomes a critical

factor at the point when a relationship develops. In long-distance dating, the development of a relationship varies from one couple to the next. Some long-distance couples decide from a week in that they are in a committed relationship, while it may take other couples months, and up to one year before they agree to a committed relationship. Whatever the case may be, when a relationship develops, decide on a timeline for the end goal of the relationship.

If you and your partner have not considered the end goal of your relationship at this point, after reading this book, you will have a better understanding of what it takes to achieve this goal. By the time you finish reading this book, you will have a clear understanding of the tools that you need to support and grow your long-distance relationship.

If you come to this book to find information that conforms to the old and outdated ways of long-distance relationships, close the book. If you are here hoping to see stories that are one cap fits all, close the book. If, however, you are looking for a new outlook on long-distance relationships, and learning new ways to build, maintain, and grow your relationship in a healthy way, keep reading. If you want to get to your end goal by learning innovative ideas and adopting useful tools, keep reading.

This book explains the components of a long-distance relationship just as it is in the real, modern world. I illustrate some of the most critical concepts in long-distance dating, with examples of what must happen in your long-distance relationship to keep your relationship moving to the next phase. With the ever-changing dynamics of relationships in the twenty-first century, this knowledge on making a long-distance relationship work is valuable, and in high demand.

After meeting the hunkiest of a man on Facebook, and instantaneously click, it finally occurred to me that I may have a thing. Fast forward to this morning, my friend called me for advice on her current long-distance relationship frustrations, and as I laid out a strategic plan of action for her about her relationship, I receive confirmation that I am overwhelmingly proficient on the topic of long-distance relationships. In all my dating, married, and divorced life, I have only dated long distance.

You will often hear people say that you must be a certain way – personality wise – to be in a long-distance relationship. While I understand this point of view, I also know that anyone can learn to function in a long-distance relationship if he or she applies the right tools to his or her relationship. The concepts that I introduce in the following pages are not hard concepts to under-stand. It is a conscious choice that you will have to make on an ongoing basis. Every day of your long-distance relationship, you will need to decide. You will decide to learn ways to advance your long-distance relationship or choose to wing it and eventually give up on the relationship. The funny thing about giving up on a long-distance relationship is that you do not feel the effects of the loss until you have let your relationship go. The pain sets in days, weeks, months, and even years after you make the decision. The point is, you will bear the pain of the loss of your relationship, especially if you did not give it your best shot.

The origin of your long-distance relationship does not matter. Whether you met in person and had to separate, or if you met online, the tools needed to build a solid foundation is still the same either way. Your relationship has the same strengths and the same weaknesses. The same strides, and the same struggles.

There is also a special section in this book for married couples who are in a long-distance marriage. Whether you married into it, or it happened after marriage due to circumstances beyond your control. Many unions have one, or both partners traveling all the time due to work; never in the same place together. This book is written to suit all types and all forms of long-distance relationships.

2
– MAINTENANCE –

Maintaining any form of relationship is hard work. Add a couple of thousand miles unto the already existing burdens of a relationship, and you will most definitely begin to think that your best choice is to give up, and not contend with a long-distance relationship. Whether you are currently struggling with this feeling, or have never struggled with it, there is undoubtedly a time when you will consider deeply, whether you can maintain a relationship of this caliber. It takes strength to commit to a long-distance relationship, and it requires even more power to support it.

To maintain your long-distance relationship, you first need to fully understand your relationship dynamics. Whether long distance or otherwise, the two people in a relationship must understand the type of relationship that they have. To maintain proper upkeep of your long-distance relationship, you must first understand how the dynamics of your relationship, affect the goals of the relationship. You must ask yourself some defining questions about your relationship, to figure out whether your current relationship dynamics is helping to elevate your relationship and the goals of your relationship, or if it is contributing to stagnancy in your relationship. This information is what you need to keep on the right track of growing a healthy long-distance relationship - one that will last.

As you begin to think about the dynamics of your relationship, consider some of the most critical aspects of the relationship. Is your relationship an open relationship, or is it exclusive? Is your relationship a seriously committed relationship, or have you ever talked about that with your partner? Is your relationship set in stone, or are you both just winging it? These are simple questions, and evident in any relationship, but people often neglect them in a long-distance relationship. Do not underestimate the need to discuss these aspects of your relationship with your partner. If you are at this point, and you realize that you are not entirely aware of these aspects of your relationship, you must make this discussion a priority before it becomes a significant issue in your relationship. Start by writing down the most critical questions that you feel will provide you with the precise answers that you need to figure out where your relationship stands. For starters, these are some sample questions that you could ask:

Are we exclusive?

What are the boundaries of our relationship?

Are we seeing other people or is it just us?

Are you in a relationship?

Are you sexually active?

One question that most people do not ask in a long-distance relationship is whether their partner is having sexual relations with other people. It mostly occurs in newly developing long-distance relationships, but there is also a considerable number of long-distance couples who are still afraid to ask these questions, even after some time has passed.

For new long-distance relationships, boundaries can be very confusing in the transition from friends to partners. Because of this, many people are not sure when it questions. Since there is no physical confirmation of the transition taking place, they are unsure of exactly when the relationships start and therefore are not sure if they need to know about these aspects of the relationship.

The physical confirmation of the transition is sex. If the change from friends to partners takes place from many miles away, the evidence of sex is visibly absent, and substitution must be imminent to complete the transformation. A verbal acknowledgment of the transition will suffice in the absence of sex. You and your partner must both verbally agree when your relationship becomes exclusive. This mutuality confirms that a connection has begun, and more importantly, it lets you know where you stand, and where your partner stands.

The verbal acknowledgment takes the guessing game out of your relationship.

When you ask these questions, you must be fully prepared to receive the answer. Prepare yourself for the best-case scenario, as well as the worst-case scenario. Expect that you may or may not get the answer that you seek. The good thing about that is, whether good or bad, everything is on display from the beginning of the relationship. This precision decreases the likelihood of secrets and lies going forward. At that point, it is then up to you to decide if and how you will move forward with the relationship.

Always keep an open and accommodating environment in your relationship; one that is conducive to honesty. In everything that you do in your life, you must be prepared to face the unexpected, and being in a long-distance relationship is no exception. Never ask a question unless you want the answer to it. Never ask for a revelation unless you are ready for a revolution. What this means is, you must always be prepared to act once you receive information. Before you ask to obtain specific information from your partner, prepare yourself for what will happen once you have the information that you requested. This preparation is a particularly useful method for damage control. Once you have gone over all the ways that your partner could respond, you are more aware of what your decision will be in the situation. The key is always to allow yourself time to process the information. A long-distance relationship can seem like a simple relationship to start, and likewise to end, but the structure of this type of relationship is much more complicated. There will always be intense moments in which you will need to make decisions that will have a high impact on your life.

Once you decide that you will tackle these tough questions with your partner, you will need to have a plan of execution. This plan will limit the likelihood that your partner receives you negatively. A gratifying approach in bringing up delicate discussions in your relationship, works hand in hand with having correct, and effective communication methods. There is no matter in your relationship that you cannot approach in a civilized manner, with an effective communication platform. To get the most favorable results, approach your partner respectfully from a space of happiness. You can achieve this by merely smiling as you speak. The more you beam; the more positivity exudes with each word that you say.

Be patient. If your partner needs more time to answer your questions, or if they are not readily available to attend to your request; be patient. The willingness to endure can mean waiting a few hours or a few days, or weeks even. You will not get the answers that you are looking for if you try to force it out of your partner. Your partner will most definitely shut down. When this occurs, it blocks communication and causes more issues in your relationship.

– The Approach –

What it comes down to is having the right timing. Things can always go right in your long-distance relationship if you learn the importance of timing. Your relationship is not a race, and you should not expect to cover everything in one day. Control the rate at which you input information into your relationship. Whether it is something that is important to know or something of less importance. Do not say too much all at once, and do not ask all your questions in one breath.

Do not bombard your partner. Build up to the most critical question, starting with a surface question. A surface question is a question that shows the direction of the conversation but does not assume anything. An example would be a question to find out the answer to whether the relationship is exclusive.

The surface question would go something like, "hey, we are doing pretty amazing at this long-distance thing, would you agree?" In this example, you are praising the effective communication that you have kept, but you are only saying just that. It is unassuming and does not give the receiving party any reason to believe that you are asking for anything. This vagueness is convenient in the case that they are not on the same page, although for your sake I hope that they are. The end of the question is open for a response from your partner. The hope is that they will lead the conversation in the desired direction. If the answer that they give is also unassuming, continue to build on your first question until you get to your desired goal. This process can take minutes, hours and even days before it lands where you intended. This unavoidable wait is where practicing patience will help you the most. Learning to be patient in these situations allows you to be airy. The ability to be airy is always good at the beginning of any relationship. It encourages both parties to act – and fast. An unintended, but a beautiful side effect of being airy is that it allows you and your partner space, in case anyone needs it for any reasons.

Maintaining your long-distance relationship is a means to an end. It is a method – a way to get you and your partner securely to the next chapter of your relationship. To achieve effective upkeep of your long-distance relationship, the word "comfortable," should never get within 500 feet of your vocabulary. If it does, your relationship will inevitably end up in hot water. Maintenance is the reason for all the effort that you put into your relationship daily. If you are in this phase of your relationship that means you have made significant sacrifices for your relationship. Take a particular interest in this. Let this be your motivation to take your relationship to the next level.

A long-distance relationship is a high-risk investment. Investments are right when they reap rewards, but they are also massive gambles. Moreover, in the case of a long-distance relationship, it is additionally volatile.

When you take extreme pride in your relationship, your eagerness to maintain it will come naturally. If you have reservations about your desire to prolong your relationship, you will find this phase frustrating and pointless. It may sound surprising to you, but the maintenance phase is neither the time nor the place to work on issues such as doubt. These kinds of problems must be isolated and resolved before you try to prolong the relationship. If you have doubts, you must take time to sort out these issues.

Do not mistake doubt for a relationship issue. It is not. Uncertainty is an individual issue. It is not logical to waste time maintaining a relationship that saturates in doubt. It drains brain power and puts an unnecessary burden on your emotional health. In the end, it will not help you, your partner, or your relationship.

– New Relationships –

New long-distance relationships are like a losing battle – literally. You will have one too many conflicts that lead to nowhere. You will question yourself on exactly why you chose to do this to yourself and will convince yourself that this "distance thing" is not for you.

This kind of thinking is what I like to describe as the thinking of a "weak link" in a relationship. A weak link is an enthusiastically self-absorbed individual in a long-distance relationship who is categorically incapable of conceptualizing things based on anyone else's point of view, except their own. In other words, they are not immediately willing to try different things to help grow their relationship, and the feelings of their partner will not influence them what-so-ever. A weak link is the least dependable person in a group. In a relationship, they cannot be depended on to give the relationship the support that it needs. They are not willing to work as hard as their partner to maintain a relationship.

As unpleasant as they sound, it is fear that controls the actions of weak links. They are highly unsure of themselves. Fear can eat at our souls if we do not find the strength to face it. Weak links are aware of this, but they lack tools with which to face their fears.

– Tools for Weak Links –

The most important concept to learn is selflessness. The number one tool that you will need going forward is openness. Open yourself to new possibilities in your relationship. If you are leery of some things, allow your partner to lead you. Share in each other's knowledge and be open to what your partner is willing to teach you.

Make a list of your needs in the relationship. This list will detail everything that you need from your partner to aide in subsiding your fears. Reveal the list to your partner and explain your reasoning for why you need each item on the list. Explain how each item will help you to become a better person in your relationship.

This exercise allows you to test the openness of your partner. You are a weak link because you have specific fears of a long-distance relationship. Your partner's responsibility in being in a relationship with you also includes helping you to overcome situations such as this one. This exercise will evaluate the strength of your relationship and the closeness of your bond with your partner. If your partner opposes any of your needs or does not provide you with the support that you need, it is a clear sign that your fears of the relationship are justifiable. Remember that not everyone whom we fall in love with is who is for us. Although the primary driving forces of your actions as a weak link are fear and frustration, do not neglect the fact that you may be right on point in some instances.

Next, embrace the realities of your relationship. Your long-distance relationship is legitimate. Act as such. Treat it as such. Regard your partner as you would if you saw them every day and slept with them in the same bed every night. Communicate with them via text, video call, email, social media, or any other medium that is convenient for you. Keep close contact to learn more about each other continuously. Build a relationship where you both can confide in each other on the areas of your relationship that you struggle with the most.

The more you do these things in your relationship, the better you will become at communicating with your partner. As you learn to communicate more effectively with your partner, and they with you, you will both discover particular mutual respect that will propel your relationship into the next phase. This new atmosphere in your relationship will ease your fears about your relationship because it removes a lot of the worrying about the survival of your relationship and instead lets you focus on building your relationship one step at a time. This relief allows you to enjoy being in the present moment of your connection and trains you on how to form a stronger bond that will become increasingly useful to the survival of your relationship as it matures.

Engage your partner in conversations like these daily. It will assure constant and open communication in your relationship. As you do this more every day, it will begin to occur to you naturally. Soon enough you and your partner will communicate effectively without having to give it a second thought. Use these opportunities to learn more about yourself and your partner. Look out for cues that will tell you if you and your partner are in fact compatible. These cues include things such as personality clashes or complements. Seek consistency. Regard all issues and situations in your relationship the same way. Build a secure system of trust where you can share feedback with each other, and practice honesty in your communication about the impending factors that are of immediate concern to you.

— *Mature/Long-Term Relationships* —

No matter how many years you have been in a long-distance relationship, the need for maintenance still is the same nonetheless. There will always be a need for more tools to continue to grow your relationship into the future. Making a deliberate effort to obtain these helpful tools is the first step in building a healthy long-distance relationship and bond with your partner. At your level of experience in your relationship, you have already learned some fundamental things about being in a long-distance relationship that you can use to help you to maintain your relationship long term. Even if you have been in your relationship for several months or several years, this does not mean that you have kept your relationship healthily. Your relationship could be holding on to the last thread even as we speak. The good news is that you can always turn this around.

There are many factors to consider when evaluating the status of your relationship. I always like to start with myself. For you to take control of any situation in your life, you must be willing to take responsibility for the part that you play. Be honest with yourself. If you can get to the point of complete honesty with yourself, then and only then, you can begin to evaluate your partner.

To work at your relationship, you need an angle. The angle is your approach. It is the role that you play and the position from which you play. Once you find your perspective, position yourself to be in control. The ideal angle that you want to be in is the one where you are open and willing to accept responsibility for the things that you have done in your relationship to either aide growth or hinder it. Position yourself to compromise on many areas of your relationship that you feel you have done well. Listen to everything that your partner has to say and listen to them keenly. Show compassion and acknowledge that you have heard their concerns and that they are essential to you. It is a rare skill to be able to agree to disagree. In a long-distance relationship, however, you must learn this, and fast.

It may or may not have occurred to you that at this point, you only have one primary tool in your relationship which is your voice. There is no other way to relate to your partner. There is no touching, no kissing, no hugging, or a warm embrace. Your voice is now the most powerful asset that you own in your relationship. Therefore, since your relationship is a huge part of your life, your voice becomes the most valuable thing in your life.

Your voice is the tool that you use to maintain your relationship. It decides the survival of your relationship. Your voice is the essence of your thinking. It is how you conceptualize things. Be extremely vigilant of what you express in your relationship and how you communicate it. Train your mind to become accustomed to the tools that you have so that those tools can project positively into your relationship. If you can be honest with yourself and accept the facts of your long-distance situation, you can focus your energy on doing the right things and using the right tools to make your relationship stronger.

Practice the act of fairness. It will benefit you to be as open and as fair as you can comfortably be, without becoming uneasy with the realities of your relationship. Being open means that you keep a constant stream of communication between you and your partner. Use the resources available to you to carry out this agenda.

Be present in your relationship. Be actively involved in the life of your partner as much as possible. Ask your partner essential questions that shows them that you have an interest in them and their lives. Show them that you care about how they are living day to day and that you think about how they eat and survive daily. Inquire about the state of their health. Encourage them to do positive things that will cause positive outcomes in their lives. Be active and present.

Be patient. If you are the type of person that always wants your way and fights relentlessly to get it, stop right now. They say patience is a virtue, and it is true. Having the ability to be patient is a valuable tool that you can use in any situation. It will work particularly well for you to allow room in your relationship for growth.

Patience is a way to show that you can reason. Practice patience in your relationship by staying calm in conversations in which you feel passionate. Show patience even if you know the facts. Show patience in times when you think you have it all figured out. If you can practice tolerance and train yourself to use this tool as a natural reaction when interacting with your partner, not only will you adopt this long-term, but your partner will respect and appreciate you for it.

Tolerance does not mean that you should bury your emotions deep into the ground. The right amount of emotional conditioning can protect the bond between you and your partner in certain situations. Some situations need a strong emotional reaction from you. When these situations occur, do not stifle your emotions. Exercise patience as a transition tool between the time you receive the information, to the moment you respond to it. You must aim to find the right balance.

It is not necessary for you to calculate everything in your long-distance relationship. You must exude control over the things that affect your life, but there is no need to obsess over them. You cannot control the behaviors that your partner display, but you can influence them. If your partner is unable to see your point of view, control the narrative and make them see your point. This approach does not guarantee that you will change their behavior or that they will listen to you, but you will undoubtedly get feedback that you can use to predict the future of your relationship.

Do not become complacent in your relationship; whether it is new, or you have been at it for a while. You will feel as if you already know everything that there is to learn about your partner and your relationship, but there is always more to determine in a long-distance relationship. Things change. Constantly. You evolve. Your partner evolves. You both live separate evolving lives. You exist in different environments that welcome change daily. You have new experiences, new interactions, and new connections daily. If all of this is happening between you, but there is no active effort from either of you to maintain your relationship, you will lose your bond as a couple, and your relationship will wither away.

Start to think of ways that you can improve your interaction with your partner. Think about what your partner's unique needs are. At this point, you should have a solid idea of the person you are with and have a good sense of what they need and expect from the relationship. As your relationship mature, you must also begin to think about what your priorities are. If you are a couple of years into your long-distance relationship, that shows that you are serious in making your relationship work long-term. It also shows that you are willing to accept the unique challenges that your relationship will face in the future as it continues to grow and mature. If this is your mindset, then you are on the right track. You have the necessities to move your relationship along. It also means that you can employ the right tools and put them to proper use in maintaining your relationship.

– Flight or Fly –

When trouble begins to set into your long-distance relationship, you will have two defense approaches from which to choose. You can fight or fly. Fight or fly gives you a choice to either fight a losing battle or find confidence within yourself to take an extraordinary step (fly) to connect with your partner. Fight or fly is precisely what the words suggest; fight each other or find the best compromise when unfortunate situations arise in your relationship.

– Fight –

Agreeing to be a part of a long-distance relationship does not mean that you accept it entirely or believe in it. You did it for love, and that is all the reason you need. However, a result of your disbelief in the foundation of a long-distance relationship, is that you stay in a state of unwillingness to find different and better ways to make your relationship arrangement work. At the same time, you are also not prepared to let the relationship go because you genuinely are in love. The desire naturally exists in you to see your relationship through to the end goal, but the realities of your relationship hinder your ability to communicate this to your partner.

When this uncertainty displays in your relationship, it causes friction. If your partner does not receive this well, these issues can swiftly blow out of proportion (fight). If you are sure of your interest in staying with your long-distance partner, you can spend your time and energy focusing on exactly how you will do it. You must allow yourself enough time to cope with the realities of a long-distance relationship.

Employing tools such as patience and operational communication is a tremendous start. Be wary of your actions and of the things that you say to your partner. Observe patterns and practice how to say yes more times than you say no to ideas in your relationship. Let your partner into your virtual space. Share your family and friends with them and familiarize them with how you live in your world. This receptivity will help you to become comfortable in your long-distance relationship.

– Fly –

Flying in a literal sense means to ascend to new heights. In a long-distance relationship, it means the same. Fly is when you make a conscious decision to turn everything in your relationship that denotes negativity and turn it into something positive. To fly, you must commit to arriving at a happy conclusion for every situation in your relationship. Resolve issues or arguments before the day ends. Engage in conversations to continually air out all problems and concerns in your relationship. Be willing to feel uncomfortable. Be wrong when you are wrong, and right when you are right. Be petrified when you are scared and talk nonsense when you are angry. Be willing to admit these uncomfortable things to move on from it and grow.

Be ambitious in your efforts to make your relationship work. You cannot come home with flowers for your partner, but you can greet them with flowers nevertheless by ordering them and having them home delivered to your partner. Be spontaneous. Decide to do as much as you can to keep your relationship advancing to the next phase.

A long-distance relationship teaches you lessons that you can apply to many aspects of your life. Maintenance is the core of your relationship and what you spend at least ninety percent of your time doing in your relationship. This phase highlights your strengths and weaknesses as an individual and forces you to function at your best in your relationship.

If you are at a point in your relationship where you are failing to maintain your bond correctly, do not panic. There is still time to fix the ills of your relationship; that is of course if your partner is willing to work at it. Start small and build up to the ideal relationship that you envision for you and your partner. Be sure to make your partner aware of your intentions to work at your relationship. The goal is to get your relationship to a point at which it is healthy, steadily functioning and growing abundantly in strength and love.

– *Communication* –

Communication is about speaking and behaving logically to connect with your partner. In a long-distance relationship, the options for discussion can become limited if you do not know how to properly conduct yourself in a manner that promotes a healthy level of communication between you and your partner. Learning how to communicate effectively is an art. The key to learning how to communicate effectively in a long-distance relationship is learning self-control. Self-control includes control of your feelings, your emotions, your reactions, your actions and most importantly, control over the things that you communicate with your partner.

The ability to keep your composure is also a skill that you will need to master to communicate effectively with your long-distance partner. Not everything that happens in your relationship calls for an action or a reaction from you. Filter the things in your relationship that are of significance to you and your partner and forget the irrelevant and otherwise unimportant factors in your relationship.

As issues arise in your relationship, approach them calmly and find a solution for them at once. Do not get into the habit of letting things settle in your relationship or leaving important issues unaddressed or questions unanswered. Doing this sets up your relationship to have these issues come up at another time in the future and bring more problems in your relationship.

Always talk things over with your partner no matter how painful or uncomfortable the topic may be. If you commit to doing this, you will experience how simple talking makes your long-distance relationship. Build up the courage to talk to your partner about tricky situations. It is never easy to approach your partner with a question or concern, but it will be harder for you if you keep it to yourself. It is torturous to have something to say at the tip of your tongue and the top of your brain but never to have the courage to say it out of your mouth. It is quite frustrating. Even more frustrating than saying it aloud could ever be.

Be readily available to meet the needs of your partner. Always be open and ready to talk to your partner about topics that you really would rather not talk about and in times when you would rather not have the discussion.

Keeping an open line of communication is just as important as learning how to be an excellent communicator. The best quality of an excellent communicator is that he or she knows that effective communication starts with an open platform. Make yourself entirely available to the needs of your partner. Make time when there is none and create space in your schedule where there is none.

– Get Rid of Your Pride –

An excellent place to start when figuring out how to effectively communicate with your partner is to understand that pride and effective communication can never coexist together in your relationship. You must let go of the prideful attributes that you have because they interfere with your ability to function in your relationship. It is not as hard as many people think it is.

Never close yourself off to your partner emotionally. Your relationship is meant to be a safe place where you can freely express your feelings, and you must not be afraid to do so. Likewise, you must create a safe environment for your partner where they can approach you with their feelings without reservation. You can achieve effective communication in your relationship by completing these simple actions daily. Do not make your relationship harder than it must be. Keep things light and on a positive note.

MAINTENANCE:
Worksheet

(Circle One):

My relationship is exclusive:

Your Answer:	Ask Partner:	Total	Total
You:	Partner:	Yes:	No:
YES | NO	YES | NO		

I can approach my partner about issues/concerns:

Your Answer:	Ask Partner:	Total	Total
You:	Partner:	Yes:	No:
YES | NO	YES | NO		

I practice fairness in my relationship:

Your Answer:	Ask Partner:	Total	Total
You:	Partner:	Yes:	No:
YES | NO	YES | NO		

I control the rate at which I input information into my relationship:

Your Answer:	Ask Partner:	Total	Total
You:	Partner:	Yes:	No:
YES | NO	YES | NO		

I have doubts about my relationship:

Your Answer:	Ask Partner:	Total	Total
You:	Partner:	Yes:	No:
YES | NO	YES | NO		

I engage my partner in gainful conversations daily:

Your Answer:	Ask Partner:	Total	Total
You:	Partner:	Yes:	No:
YES | NO	YES | NO		

I am actively involved in my partner's life:

Your Answer:	Ask Partner:	Total	Total
You:	Partner:	Yes:	No:
YES | NO	YES | NO		

I exercise patience in my relationship:

Your Answer:	Ask Partner:	Total	Total
You:	Partner:	Yes:	No:
YES | NO	YES | NO		

I am readily available to meet the needs of my partner:

Your Answer:	Ask Partner:	Total	Total
You:	Partner:	Yes:	No:
YES | NO	YES | NO		

Answer Guide:

YES	NO
8	1

Notes:

3
– PULL PUSH PRINCIPLE –

The pull principle and push principle refers to the level of emotional openness that you and your partner share in your relationship. It is a measure of the level of emotional resistance that exists in your relationship. The pull, push, paralyze phases are a result of your emotional reactions, as well as the experiences behind those emotions. You can think of it as a road map that traces all your emotional experiences – good and bad – and creates a summary of what you have been through in your life.

– Pull –

The ideal form of a long-distance relationship is a pull scenario. In this scenario, both parties are pulling equal weights in the relationship, and they both find pleasure in doing so. The pull phase is like the honeymoon phase on steroids. It needs a firm commitment from both you and your partner to keep it going. In the pull stage, you are open to your partner. You want to learn as much about them as you can and as quickly as you can. You get butterflies in your stomach as you think about the possibilities of your long-term relationship, and you know in your gut that you are in love or could be in love.

If your partner is in the pull phase along with you, your relationship becomes bliss momentarily. I say momentarily because as human beings, we continue to change and evolve over time and so do our relationships. We fall in and out and back into love continually. It is like breathing - a natural occurrence. The responsibility will always remain with you and your partner to keep this bond in your relationship.

If your partner is in a pull phase, they will offer you themselves openly. This level of openness and honesty will excite you and alarm you at the same time. Your partner will show immense interest in wanting to understand you and to find out everything about you that is important for them to know. They will want in on your family history, your likes, and dislikes and other vital details about your existence.

They will also ask you about your most recent relationship. When your partner asks this question, they are actively seeking a way to let you know that they care about all aspects of your life and that they intend to do right by you. It is a way for them to invite you to open to them and to form a trusting bond with them. Their aim in doing this is for you to relieve yourself of your reservations and be open to the idea of trusting them. In a perfect scenario, they hope that you decide to open to them (pull) and establish a common ground, but that does not happen in every case.

You may have some reservations about telling your new partner about your old partner for fear that it will set a negative tone in your relationship and you are not wrong for thinking in this way. Whenever the past is brought up in a relationship disaster tends to happen. The information may turn in ways that it was not meant to, or it may be used against you further down the line. These are all possibilities, but they should not be your primary concern. Sharing information about your past relationship with your new partner does have the potential to go wrong, but that is only if you let it. If you are always in control of the information that you input into your relationship, you keep permanent control over the impact that it creates in your relationship. The key is to limit and regulate the information that you put into your relationship.

The pull and push dynamics continues indefinitely. It can occur from day to day or hour to hour in your relationship. It is up to you and your partner to continuously make an effort to keep your relationship intact. In a long-distance relationship you both depend on each other, and so you both must equally work to keep your relationship functioning and growing.

– Pull Push –

In this scenario, your relationship becomes unbalanced because one or both of you have stopped putting effort into your relationship. Something went wrong. It could be anything such as an argument or knowledge of the past or a severe conflict of interest.

Arguments: Most couples dread the first argument in a long-distance relationship, mainly because they find it easy to end the relationship with the least amount of emotional investment. Some of us can handle certain situations better than others and so something that you may have said to hurt your partner may be hurtful to you if the roles reverse. Likewise, what your partner said to hurt you, will more than likely hurt them if the positions change. The extent of the impact on your relationship becomes buried if you both focus on whom to blame instead of resolving the primary cause of the issues.

If this confusion continues for longer than it should, it will decide the faith of your relationship. The uncertainty creates triggers in your relationship that becomes a constant source of conflict between you and your partner. These triggers come from two places - your principles and your past experiences.

Principles: As you go through life, you become more aware of the dynamic relationships around you. These include relationships such as that of your mom and dad, or even the lack thereof, such as an absentee mom or dad or both. Depending on the environment that you grew up in, the principles you adopt decide how you make decisions in your relationship. Although, so long as we are living, breathing organisms, we are inevitably and eternally guaranteed to experience changes. Our principles will continue to evolve as we grow. Think about it. How many new experiences have you had over the past week? How many of them have changed your life in some way? How much impact has these changes have on your governing principles? Have your beliefs changed since your experience reading this book? Change is unavoidable. Do not fear it. Embrace it.

Past Experiences: Triggers may also come from our past experiences. Yes, you know the one I am talking. That one bad break up or that one bad falling out with your close family or friend. Every experience, good or bad, that we have had throughout our entire lives up until this current moment has created a psychological road map of our rationale. If you are deciding, you can use this map of your experiences to reveal the depths of your reasoning and uncover the motives for why you take the actions that you do, specifically as it relates to your emotional reactions in your relationship. You must assess your reasoning abilities before you try to function in a long-distance relationship. This type of relationship needs you to generate an elevated level of trust, and you must achieve this; otherwise your relationship will become too complicated for you to manage. Assess the thought process that you usually engage before you react to a situation in your relationship. Do this on a continuous basis until you produce an effective way to decipher your emotions when emotionally demanding situations arise in your relationship.

If you can train your mind in this way, you will find that you engage in fewer arguments that are based on things that happened in the past and learn to embrace the present. People need to have a good sense of self for the world to keep functioning well. When we are unable to achieve this on our own, we employ the help of professionals. I am a firm believer in self-help. I believe in self-help now more than ever because I am living, breathing proof, that you can train your mind in ways that help you and allows you to achieve your desires.

Knowledge of the past: Call it whatever you may, but there are certain things about your past relationships that you do not have to share with your current partner. If you are wondering if I am suggesting that you lie to your partner, the answer is it depends. Withholding information about things you have done in your past does not constitute a lie unless your partner was a victim in that past, or if the past event can affect the present or the future of your relationship. It does not matter if there is any proof or not, if it has the potential to change your current relationship, you must reveal it to your partner before they find out from someone else or from somewhere else. If it is substantial enough that you describe it as a secret, you must reveal it to your partner. If the problem is something that you could talk about over beer and chips at game night, then let it be.

Conflict of interest: I am sure you did not need this book to tell you that you should always be aware of the people you are involved with, whether romantically or otherwise. A conflict of interest in your relationship is a mutual person of interest. This person is anyone who poses a unique and immediate threat to your relationship. If you and your partner cross the threshold and declare your relationship and then something like this happens, it may severely damage or completely ruin your relationship.

These interests include individuals such as your exes and anyone who is a fan of your past relationships. These people pose a unique threat to your relationship because they create distractions in your relationship that may interfere with the bond that you try to build with your partner. Some of these revelations can be critical indicators for whether the relationship is likely to work long-term, but this is not a healthy way to arrive at this conclusion.

These revelations become life altering because once you are aware of them, it is impossible to ignore them. They become real problems, and you must sacrifice certain aspects of your relationship to avoid further chaos. If this happens, you must apply damage control by talking through the entire issue with your partner before the situation explodes. Worst case scenario, your relationship does not survive. It is fair to say that the universe has its way of putting these things in order as they should be. Do not try to force something to work that was not meant to work.

They say that prevention is better than cure. To avoid getting into this predicament, take early precautions to eradicate these threats from your relationship. If you are aware of something that may be detrimental to your relationship or if there is a significant conflict of interest that you know will not work itself out, address it with your partner. Do not wait until it is too late to pursue the issue. It will be emotional suicide.

Whenever the circumstances of your long-distance relationship cause you to have persistent reservations about your relationship, it is natural for you to act on these feelings. Consequently, your partner may have an adverse reaction to this which will inescapably send your relationship down an unstable path. The level of emotional openness in your relationship decides what the outcome of your relationship will be long-term.

After spending quality time to resolve issues that come up in your relationship, a substantial amount of your mental and emotional energy expels, leaving an unfavorable impact on your ability to function in your relationship. This drain will cause you to shut down emotionally.

Do not underestimate the amount of effort that you must continually put into your relationship. You will begin to see that it is a never-ending cycle of managing feelings and emotions, handling issues and concerns, and making good after arguments and disagreements. It is usually after this realization when most long-distance couples begin to give up. Their commitment to their relationship stays the same, and they still feel the same way about their partner, but at the same time, they do not have any desire to contribute anything more to the relationship.

This ordeal happens to the best of us. It happens whether you are in a new long-distance relationship or a mature long-distance relationship. When this happens, it is ok for you to take some time to recuperate. Express it to your partner. Do not panic over it. Take a moment and evaluate your relationship. It does not need to alter the foundation of your relationship. It does not mean that you call your partner up and tell them that the relationship is not working. It means that you keep communication with your partner about the concerns that you have and find a mutual solution. The whole time, you are continuing to keep the connection that you have with them and actively try to move your relationship forward. Think about the things that weigh heavily on your mind outside of your relationship. Also, think regarding the things that prevent you from committing wholeheartedly to the idea of being in a long-distance relationship. Some of these things include family, friends, and other influencers in your life.

– *Emotional Health* –

To begin to take care of your emotional health, invest heavily in your wellbeing. Make it a routine to do something special for yourself on a weekly basis outside of your relationship. Doing this on a regular basis will replenish your mind of a lot of the things that you lose due to the strains of a long-distance relationship. These include things such as your peace of mind, happiness, and sense of self. Doing this enables you to function well in your long-distance relationship.

Do not take this lightly. Maintaining proper physical, mental and emotional health while in a long-distance relationship is essential. Considering the facts of a long-distance relationship, you are physically alone most of the time, and so it is critical that you invest in your wellbeing before trying to invest in your partner.

This concept is simple. You must take care of your own needs before you will ever be able to take care of someone else's. When you are on an airplane, and they give you instructions on how to proceed in the case of an emergency, they instruct you to ensure that your mask is secure before trying to help anyone else.

In fact, it is not even a choice; it is a requirement. Unfortunately, in life, we do not have such a requirement and so we must learn how to do this on our own. There is only so much you can do to help others if you are suffocating to death. If you apply this analogy to your relationship, you will get a better understanding of why it is crucial for you to protect and secure your wellbeing before aiming to do so for your partner. Let this analogy be a constant reminder to you of who is more important in any given situation.

However, is it selfish? Absolutely. If you do not learn to take care of your psychological health when you are in a long-distance relationship, many things will go wrong in your personal life as well as in your relationship. Take care of the distractions in your life. Focus entirely on inputting good energy into your long-distance relationship. Ninety percent of this energy will be you trying to cope with the reality of your relationship, while the other ten percent is you actively taking part in the relationship.

Since you spend most of your energy finding different strategies to cope with the reality that you are not with the one you love, it is essential to keep everything that affects you emotionally at a healthy distance. These emotional factors do not have to be anything that is related to your relationship. In fact, in many instances, it is the outside factors such as work, family, and the other social and personal influencers in your life that demands the most emotional contribution from you.

– *Push* –

When you begin to push in your relationship, it is not only a result of the pressures in your relationship, but it can also be a direct response from outside influences on your relationship. Limit those influences at once. Stop asking for advice on your relationship. Stop letting the opinions of external factors cloud your judgment. I assure you that aside from what is taking place in your relationship, the other factors at play in your relationship are the outside influencers that you allow to think for you. Indeed, you should not shut out everyone in your surroundings for the sake of your relationship. Some of these people can be healthy for you if they offer constructive advice to you on matters of your relationship. What you must do is choose what information you take and what information you do not. Take control of what you allow to influence your thoughts and actions.

The pull and push phases are reoccurring, and there is no specific order to which they recycle themselves. You may experience these phases at separate times, depending on the level of change that is happening in your relationship. These phases are what tells you whether you have a healthy emotional bond with your partner. If your relationship continually recycles these phases, that says that there are too many additional events taking place in your relationship at the same time. Too many outside influencers are having an influence on either you, your partner or both of you at the same time. You may be aware of some of these influences, but most of them tend to creep up on your relationship and bring confusion with them. You and your partner will blame each other for what is happening in your relationship and will expect each other to fix the issues individually. In the meantime, the significant problems and threats continue to lurk around your relationship.

Couples that fail at fixing problems in their relationship do not fail because they cannot come to a permanent resolution to the problem. They fail because they are using the wrong methods to solve the problem. It is not normal for a relationship to recycle these phases on a frequent basis. If this is happening in your relationship, you and your partner must make a joint effort to remedy it at once. If this is happening in your relationship, it does not mean that your relationship is hopeless. There is much friction in your relationship that is causing confusion and tensions between you and your partner and that is never an ideal situation in any relationship. You may not even engage in verbal altercations or arguments, but the emotions within you control the way you interact with your partner. As your long-distance relationship matures, you will come to find out that a lot of the times you will become trapped inside your head. The realities of your relationship will continuously create an avenue of confusion for you that will affect the bond between you and your partner in one way or the other. Take control of situations that affect your relationship by having standards that govern your beliefs about your relationship. Create rules for your relationship, so you know what is worth paying attention to and what is not.

Think regarding the influencers of your relationship. Who are the influencers in your relationship? Do they provide you with constructive advice to enhance your relationship? Is it by your standards to consider the opinions of these influencers? What happens if you decide to ignore them? What would the implications be in that case?

***

Use a strict form of critical analysis in evaluating concepts that apply to your relationship. Being able to think through these factors critically will allow you to have a better understanding of the influences in your relationship. Being in a long-distance relationship is a repetitive cycle. You will only endure if you possess determination and patience to deal with the constant recycling of changes and issues in your relationship. Many of the problems that you face or will face in your long-distance relationship are fixable. The good thing about these issues that come up in your relationship is that they continuously recycle themselves. If you pay very close attention to your relationship, you will notice these issues and squash them before they get a chance to engrave in your relationship. Soon enough, conflict management will become like second nature to you.

There is always an effective way to collaborate with your partner on ways to enhance your long-distance relationship work and make it last long term. Take the time to find ways to cut unimportant factors from your relationship. Evaluate different factors against your standards to decide what factors are worth pursuing and what factors are irrelevant in your relationship. Internalize these factors and try to resolve them before bringing them into your relationship.

PULL PUSH PRINCIPLE:

Worksheet

(Circle One)

I am open to my partner:

Your Answer:	Ask Partner:	Total	Total
You:	Partner:	Yes:	No:
YES | NO	YES | NO		

I interpret my emotions well in emotionally demanding situations in my relationship:

Your Answer:	Ask Partner:	Total	Total
You:	Partner:	Yes:	No:
YES | NO	YES | NO		

I have immediate knowledge of something that could be detrimental to my relationship:

Your Answer:	Ask Partner:	Total	Total
You:	Partner:	Yes:	No:
YES | NO	YES | NO		

I engage in social activity outside of my relationship:

Your Answer:	Ask Partner:	Total	Total
You:	Partner:	Yes:	No:

YES | NO	YES | NO		

I input good energy into my relationship:

Your Answer:	Ask Partner:	Total	Total
You:	Partner:	Yes:	No:
YES | NO	YES | NO		

I have standards that I use to govern my beliefs about my relationship:

Your Answer:	Ask Partner:	Total	Total
You:	Partner:	Yes:	No:
YES | NO	YES | NO		

My relationship continually recycles the pull and push phases:

Your Answer:	Ask Partner:	Total	Total
You:	Partner:	Yes:	No:
YES | NO	YES | NO		

I am always frustrated by my relationship:

Your Answer:	Ask Partner:	Total	Total
You:	Partner:	Yes:	No:

YES | NO	YES | NO		

Answer Guide:

YES	NO
5	3

Notes:

4
− THINK CRITICALLY −

To master critical thinking in your long-distance relationship, you must comprehend that you and your partner think in separate ways on different days. Every day of your lives brings out something new in you. As the time passes by in your long-distance relationship, it becomes harder to track these changes because you spend most of your time being physically out of touch with each other. It is no secret that couples who can connect face to face daily learn important things about each other much faster than those in a long-distance relationship. Being face to face affords real-time information on how your partner is doing and records their real-time reaction when things develop in the relationship. In a long-distance relationship, you must work harder to understand your partner since distance is a factor in the relationship.

Every day of our lives we use stories to guide us in the decisions we take. These stories can be of the past, present or future. What is most important is the impact that they leave on our lives. Our thoughts are only as impactful as the influence it has on the decisions we make. It is what inspires us to seek purpose in our lives. To properly function in a long-distance relationship, it will take mental strength and resilience. If you have been at this for a while, you understand better than anyone else that it is not easy to maintain a long-distance relationship. It is a repeated cycle of always seeking help in figuring things out.

The right thing to do in a long-distance relationship changes often. There are always exceptions and diverse ways of handling the same situation. It is as if we are making our own rules as we go along. It is incredibly unique how long-distance relationships work. You can love it or hate it, or you can appreciate it or stay away from it. It is solely up to you. Make a conscious decision on what you feel is right for you. Make this decision based on where you are in your life currently and where you would like to be long- term. Falling in love is quite easy – more accessible than most are willing to admit. It is the challenging work that comes after falling in love that discourages many people from forming this bond on a permanent basis.

I have grown into the world of long-distance dating and have watched the dynamics of it change in front of my eyes. Long distance relationships are incredibly fruitful relationships that can provide you with most if not all the general components that you would ordinarily find in a regular relationship. Long distance relationships are dynamic, and with the correct approach and practical tools, you can make it through the hard phases of your long-distance relationship and achieve your end goal in a happy, healthy, and flourishing relationship. The key is to preserve faith in your bond as a couple, and never stop believing in the foundations of your relationship.

– The Approach –

As you continue to think about the foundation of your long-distance relationship, you must have a thought progression by which you follow. This idea is common sense in all other aspects of our lives, yet many people neglect to take this direct approach to their relationship. Most believe that since their relationship is personal, it is also casual. If you think this way about your long-distance relationship, you will have multiple issues to face in your relationship further down the line. To begin to think seriously about the future of your long-distance relationship, use the following questions as guides to redirect your thoughts:

What are the goals of the relationship?

What problems do you face in achieving these goals?

What aspects of your relationship are most important in achieving these goals?

What is the purpose of wanting to achieve these goals?

Who advocates this purpose?

– What are the goals of the relationship? –

People usually do not enter a long-distance relationship just for fun – at least ordinary people do not. A long-distance relationship is not an avenue to escape boredom. If you choose to be in a long-distance relationship, you must have somehow thought of what an end goal would be. Long distance relationships are successful when they have solid goals. It is a never-ending cycle of setting goals and following through with them. In a long-distance relationship couples set dates in advance for when they will meet face to face. The couples who are seriously committed to a future together map out their plans for marriage including the time, place, and way it will happen. These all constitute goals in a long-distance relationship.

For your long-distance relationship to make sense to you, your partner or to anyone else for that matter, there must be a logical plan in place for what you want to happen in your relationship. I can inform you from experience that it is quite easy to get lost and caught up in the "now" in a long-distance relationship that you forget that there is supposed to be a "later." In fact, a lot of long-distance couples get complacent because they are experiencing temporary happiness and pleasure from the relationship. However, that is just it. The joy they are experiencing right now in the relationship, as they live unconcernedly enjoying each other without a thought for tomorrow, is all temporary. What you do not want to end up happening is to figure this out when it is too late to try and fix it. As such, you must have a plan in place of how you will make your happiness remain permanent in your long-distance relationship.

As you continue to think about your relationship, think about what the future goals are for your relationship. Engage your partner in conversation about your thoughts and get their input on what their goals are for the relationship. As you share and exchange goals with each other, try to agree on what the best course of action will be in your relationship to get to your end goal. This plan must be mutually favorable to the life you both envision for yourselves.

Create a list of goals together that you both believe in and that you both want for yourselves as individual as well as for your relationship. As you set goals in your relationship, continue to work as partners in following through with those goals. Use this time as a time to bond with each other and to grow through the stages of your relationship goals.

— What problems do you face in achieving these goals? —

Focus solely on creating your goals first. Once you and your partner have set goals for your relationship, the next step will be to execute these goals. In a perfect world, we can make and carry out goals as we please with no interruptions or setbacks. Unfortunately, we do not live in this ideal world. In the world that we do live in, there is always one setback after the other that make our goals seem impossible the closer we try to get to them. In a long-distance relationship, the key is always to be one step ahead of those setbacks. By planning for delays in advance, you have the advantage of knowing all of how an attack could happen on the foundation of your relationship, and you and your partner can be prepared to face them head-on.

Plan for Setbacks. The way you go about planning is for you and your partner to sit and talk through any setback that you could possibly face as a couple as you move forward with your goals. Do not leave anything to chance. Put every aspect of your relationship on the table for discussion no matter how much the idea may scare you or make you uncomfortable. A good example is a discussion about family. If your prime concern is about the acceptance of your relationship by family, do not be afraid to say it. Another example is the dreaded discussion on children. For instance, if you are against having children, but your partner wants ten kids, this would be a significant pitfall in your relationship. You cannot ignore a complication as substantial as this, mainly if your plans include marriage and children. Do not leave anything unsaid in these discussions as your relationship could face multiple setbacks and may or may not recover.

Once you see the potential for problems and drawbacks in your relationship, plan for how you will resolve them as they come along. When you train yourself to be this efficient at naming and preparing for issues in your relationship it becomes habitual and something that you will begin to do as you grow in your relationship. You and your partner must make a conscious effort to practice and train each other on how to spot issues in your relationship which poses a threat to your lifelong goals. You must both formulate a plan of execution for how you will eliminate problems in your relationship long before they come up.

Unnecessary Issues. Do not create unnecessary issues in your relationship or try to fix a problem that does not exist. It seems like common sense now, and you are thinking to yourself that you are not naïve to start an unnecessary conflict in your relationship, but most couples who do this daily are not aware that they are doing it. At some point or another, we have had discussions with our partner and have taken something small and insignificant from the debate and used it to create an argument sometime after. This is how you create unnecessary conflict in your relationship. You cannot plan for these issues. There is no conceivable way of knowing when they will happen because you create them.

– What aspects of your relationship are most important in achieving these goals? –

The next question that you want to ask yourself is what areas of your life you will need to focus on or alter to achieve the goals that you and your partner have set out for your relationship. It is fair to expect that we will need to change some things about ourselves when we enter a relationship. We usually learn things such as sharing and caring for someone else and learning how to be accountable and take responsibility for our actions. The added constraints of being away from your partner make it even harder to construct these changes in a long-distance relationship.

The aspects of your life that are important to your goals do not necessarily have to be things that you need to change. It can also be the things that you need to embrace. Look at it as a form of self-reflection and a time to dig deep and figure out what you genuinely want from your relationship.

It is always wise to discuss these critical factors with your relationship partner; however, it is also necessary that you take time to analyze your wants and needs. Many of us do not connect with our inner desires, and that is still the number one reason for conflict in our relationships. The one persistent thing in our life is change. It is the only thing that is sure to happen. We experience many changes in our lives, and so we must always make a conscious effort to remain connected with what our true desires are. When you connect to your desires, you are more likely to find the aspects of your life that are important in achieving the goals of your relationship.

– What is the purpose of wanting to achieve these goals? –

The purpose is the single most prominent driving force behind everything that we do in our lives. Every action that we take has a purpose. This purpose is what we hope to achieve. Whether the reason we do a particular activity is a good reason or not, the mission still justifies the action. For a goal to mean something, there must be a purpose for the goal. It is not usually the first choice that people decide to be in a long-distance relationship. For those of us who would change the situation immediately if we had the power to, there is a higher purpose for why we want to continue in our relationship and for why we want to achieve our end goal. Your purpose for being in a long-distance relationship transcends the goals that you set in your relationship. If you do not have a purpose for being in your relationship, you will not have a reason to achieve any of your relationship goals. In fact, you will not have a reason or desire to do anything much in the relationship. Your purpose for being in your relationship decides the outcome of your relationship.

If you struggle to find purpose in your relationship, you must have a conversation with your partner at once. I know many people in life who practice self-sacrificing, and I do not wish for any of my readers to become a part of that perpetual self-sacrificing business. Self-sacrifice happens when you care about the needs of others more than your own needs. You must dig deep to find the purpose. If you are at a point in your life where this thought confuses you, then you must step back from the needs of your relationship and focus on your own needs as an individual. This self-evaluation is what you need to find purpose in your long-distance relationship.

– Who advocates this purpose? –

When you satisfy your individual needs, you can

maintain your happiness while experiencing happiness with your partner. It is after you find your joy that you can indulge in the delight that everyone else tries to create for you. Always maintain your independence even as a part of a relationship that calls for a lot of togetherness and communication. Always find the time to analyze your thoughts. It is effortless to neglect the usefulness of your thoughts when you do not exercise them. Ensure that the purpose that you stand by is something that you firmly believe. Confirm that the goals are what you believe in and would support. As time goes by you will evolve and change, as will the things that you want and the things that you will and will not tolerate.

It is crucial that you continuously nurture the goals that you and your partner set for your relationship. If your feelings change at any point and for any reason, it is in your best interest to speak up about those changes. Do not ignore this. You do not want at any point to have the goals of your relationship dictated for you or to have the purpose of those goals prescribed for you. That is a sure way to cause a lifetime worth of conflict in your relationship.

If you have been on autopilot in your relationship, it is high time you stepped up and take some control over what happens in your relationship. It is neither fun nor convenient for you to allow your relationship to materialize without your consent. Take control of the things that affect you, and that changes your life. Understand that your relationship is as serious as any. If you are doing serious things and making serious plans, you cannot afford to sit back and let your partner or someone else control what happens in your relationship.

The idea of critical thinking in your long-distance relationship is about using a thorough thought process to make wise decisions in your relationship. A long-distance relationship needs much dedication from you concerning your effort, and so if you can reason about situations concerning your relationship, you will be able to navigate seamlessly through all the other aspects of your relationship. As you transition forward , always remember the goals that you set up in question one. Continually evaluate yourself to ensure that you still believe in those goals. Address new challenges as they come up and stay on top of all aspects of your relationship.

THINK CRITICALLY:

Worksheet

I practice critical thinking about my relationship:

Your Answer:	Ask Partner:	Total	Total
You:	Partner:	Yes:	No:
YES | NO	YES | NO		

I have determined an end goal for my relationship:

Your Answer:	Ask Partner:	Total	Total
You:	Partner:	Yes:	No:
YES | NO	YES | NO		

There is a logical plan in place for what will happen in my relationship:

Your Answer:	Ask Partner:	Total	Total
You:	Partner:	Yes:	No:
YES | NO	YES | NO		

I frequently engage my partner in conversation about the future of our relationship:

Your Answer:	Ask Partner:	Total	Total
You:	Partner:	Yes:	No:
YES | NO	YES | NO		

The goals of my relationship match my individual goals for my life:

Your Answer:	Ask Partner:	Total	Total
You:	Partner:	Yes:	No:
YES | NO	YES | NO		

I leave a lot of things unsaid in my relationship:

Your Answer:	Ask Partner:	Total	Total
You:	Partner:	Yes:	No:
YES | NO	YES | NO		

I create unnecessary issues in my relationship:

Your Answer:	Ask Partner:	Total	Total
You:	Partner:	Yes:	No:
YES | NO	YES | NO		

I struggle to find purpose in my relationship:

Your Answer:	Ask Partner:	Total	Total
You:	Partner:	Yes:	No:
YES | NO	YES | NO		

My partner or someone else controls what happens in

my relationship:

Your Answer:	Ask Partner:	Total	Total
You:	Partner:	Yes:	No:
YES | NO	YES | NO		

Answer Guide:

YES	NO
5	4

Notes:

5
– DAY TO DAY –

Breathe. To get through day to day in a long-distance relationship, you must learn the art of breathing in and breathing out. Go ahead, take a moment, and breathe in and out. How do you feel? If you can learn to do this, you will have a much better time handling the realities of your relationship and will spend a significantly less amount of time engaging in unnecessary conflict with your partner. I say it is unnecessary because, in a long-distance relationship, we are inclined to do things out of boredom. When our minds tell us that it needs entertainment we start a conversation with our partner on a topic that we care nothing about and cause unnecessary conflict in our relationship. Many of us are guilty of doing this. The intention is not to create conflict, but the conflict is always the result of doing it. The funny thing about life is that it has a way of twisting things, making them either for us or against us.

We do many unnecessary things out of boredom in a long-distance relationship. We find ourselves alone most of the time, and we crave for human attention. That is just a natural thing about human beings. One of the more frequent reasons why we act out in our long-distance relationship is that we are sexually frustrated. Even the well-conditioned like myself, cannot escape this in a long- distance relationship – it just happens. We are all prone to having these feelings.

Whatever the reasons may be, when boredom strikes us we tend to act out and cause conflict in our relationship. Some of us even find it entertaining to do so. Some persons find comfort in keeping their partner on their toes by playing mind games with them. Some do it leisurely while others use extreme measures to perform dangerous mind tricks on their partner. When they do this, they believe that they are exuding control in the relationship. That sense of power gives them comfort in knowing that their partner is always loyal. It is like insecurity on steroids and is by no means ok. If you have been doing this for a while, years even, you are convincing yourself right now that you do not know what I am saying and that you can do whatever you want. Whatever the case may be, I am pleading with you to stop now. If you continue on this path, you risk losing your relationship.

Aside from the fact that it is distasteful to continue doing these acts, it is also a form of psychological abuse. It is a common characteristic of a long-distance relationship to have struggles daily but resorting to these kinds of extreme coping methods is wrong and inexcusable. If your partner becomes aware of what you are doing, you can be sure that your relationship will come to a halt instantly.

There are many ways to cope with the day to day struggles of your long-distance relationship. The first in that list of things is to talk directly to your partner about how you are feeling. Communication is key. It is of absolute importance in a long-distance relationship. You will find from experience that the smallest loophole in your communicative method with your partner is always enough room for conflict to grow in your relationship. An effective method to combat this is always to ensure that you leave nothing to chance.

The day to day of a long-distance relationship can be miserable; that I can readily admit. However, what I must also tell you about are the days that are magnificent. Those days that make you fall in love with your partner all over again many times in the same day. The days that reminds you that the distance between you and your partner is well worth it because your partner gives you something that money cannot buy. This beautiful feeling is what carries you from day to day in your relationship and inspires you never to give up, regardless of how you feel in a given moment.

If you linger on these good feelings at the moment when they happen, you can build up enough coping energy to carry you over to the next time you see your partner. I believe in the power of the human mind. It can take you places without you ever physically being in that place. When your thoughts become extreme, they can connect you with your partner. Use concentration to magnify the connection. These perfect days in a long-distance relationship are always worth mentioning

because they give hope to everyone who finds themselves in love from a distance. Although your thoughts
cannot hold you at nights or hug you when you are
upset, the feelings that develop inside of you becomes
enough to substitute the need for those things.

The things that many of us struggle within the day to
day of our long-distance relationship are things that we
can readily work on and fix at once. Some of these issues include having speaker's block - not knowing what
to say any more; struggling with the repetitiveness of
your relationship, losing interest in your relationship,
and struggles to keep the romance alive in your relationship.

– Speaker's Block –

One of the biggest misconceptions about a long-distance
relationship is that there is a requirement to talk to your
partner all day every day or the relationship dissolves. I
am not sure who set these standards or created these
rules. You need to talk to your partner at least once per
day, if possible, but it is not a cause for a freak-out if
this does not happen multiple times in a day. Further-
more, you should not have to worry about running out
of things to say. The good news is you are not alone.
Many long-distance couples struggle with this very
same thing daily. It is ok to have certain days in your
relationship when it is going to be hello and goodbye or
good morning and goodnight. It does not mean that
you have completely lost interest in your partner or that
your partner has lost interest in you. It happens often.

You will inescapably experience speaker's block at one point or another in your long-distance relationship. This behavior comes with that territory. Many people in long-distance relationships today still follow an uninformed and out-of-date version of advice about long-distance relationships. In pursuing this old advice, they become paranoid when they find that nothing inspires them to talk about with their partner on a specific day. In the modern world of long-distance relationships pacing is everything. In your day to day conversations with your partner, do not try to do the most. When you speak to your partner, your topics should be few and substantial. You can have a conversation all day with your partner on the very same subject if you are skilled enough. However, you must master the art of holding someone's attention, or this will be extremely hard for you to do.

Few. There are many detours when having a conversation. Questions always lead to other questions and thoughts offshoot other thoughts. Find one topic each day that can last for hours, if not the entire day. When you master doing this, it will become easy for you to not only have things to talk about, but you will always find inspiration for further conversation as you go along. This technique limits the number of times you experience blockage in thought or speech.

Substantial. With everything that there is to learn about each other, it is a mystery how long-distance couples experience scarcity in things to say. Aim to discuss essential elements of your relationship. Something as simple as asking how your partner's day at work was or what they did that day. It is substantial and can spark an extended conversation between you about how you are both coping in your daily lives without each other. Talk about the future. Talk about your plans to see each other and all the things you will do and places you will go together. Plan constantly. Talk about family, about your dreams and aspirations and your plans for your future. Always remember that it is ok to not talk about anything on some days as well. It is common in long-distance relationships, and it should not take away from your relationship or cause you to lose interest in your partner or your relationship.

– Repetitive –

If your complaint about your long-distance relationship is the repetitiveness, I cannot debate with you on that because the day to day of a long-distance relationship is repetitive by design. It is because of this fact, why it is vital for you to understand and to accept the realities of your relationship. In every long-distance relationship, there is a familiar pattern and design. Your options for communication with your partner are constant. You speak on the phone, text, or send things in the mail to each other. On a regular basis, you ask each other about the day you had, you talk about your relationship and everything concerning your relationship, and you make plans. This is the reality of a long-distance relationship. Not much will change drastically in the relationship while you are physically apart.

The issue of repetitiveness is not so much about finding ways to remedy it. You must allow yourself to accept that this is what will happen in your relationship while you are apart. The repetitiveness helps you to transition from day to day, week to week, month to month and year to year for as long as you are physically away from your partner. You must acknowledge the good about repetition before you can appreciate what it does to improve your relationship.

If you can accept repetition as a regular part of your long-distance relationship, you are in an advantageous position. Repetition is an unfavorable word for consistency. In a long-distance relationship, repetition helps you to be consistent in your interactions with your partner and allows you to become more effective at solving issues as they come up in your relationship. You learn to be consistent in the things that you say to your partner as well as the things you ordinarily do in your relationship. When you study these things, you can see what is working in your relationship and what is not working and can remedy them. Apart of the repetition in a long-distance relationship is the repetition of the conflicts that come up in the relationship. On the surface, this seems like a disadvantage rather than an advantage, however, as these issues repeat themselves you grow more immune to them.

To curve repetitiveness, look for things that you can do differently in your interaction with your partner that will change the outcome of your conversations positively. Be spontaneous in as many ways as you can. Say new and surprising things that will be pleasing for your partner to hear. If there is something that your partner has always wanted you to do for them, consider trying it if it is something that you are comfortable doing.

Be spontaneous. There are many things that you can do, based on the type of relationship that you have, to become more spontaneous in your day to day interactions with your partner. Study your partner extremely well. Appreciate the things that your partner finds interest in and be faithful in your efforts to connect with them on a deeper level each day. Not only will this satisfy your day to day communication needs, but it will also help you and your partner to grow more intimately. Putting in this effort shows your partner that you have an interest in the relationship. If you are putting in this type of energy on a regular basis, when those slow days happen in your relationship, you can relax knowing you have sowed good seeds in your relationship. If you cannot readily find things to talk about go with the flow and do not beat yourself up or begin to wonder if your relationship is working out. Do not panic. Breathe.

– Losing interest –

Loss of interest is one of the biggest and most confusing things to try to figure out in a long-distance relationship. If you feel like you are losing interest in your relationship, there are several reasons why that may be happening and several ways that you can work on it. A lot of the times when interest fades in a long-distance relationship, it is because one or both people involved do not see a future in the relationship. Who can blame them? If I did not see a future in a relationship, I would begin to lose interest as well. It is irrational to expect to invest time, and energy in a relationship that you will spend the better part of your life, or even worst, your entire life apart. If there is a permanent barrier that you know will prevent you from ever being together with your partner and you begin to lose interest over this, the best way to go about dealing with the situation is to talk to your partner and find a resolution to the problem.

Do not rule out the fact that the decision may be an agreement between both of you to end your relationship. You must prepare yourself because this is indeed a possibility.

If, however, there is not a permanent barrier that you foresee that will prevent you from being with your partner in the future, then your loss of interest may be because of uncertainty with where your relationship stands. In this case, you must work on making the future for your relationship clear with your partner. Talk to your partner and let them know that you have concerns about how you will both go about planning for your future. Go over different possibilities with them of how you will both execute your future together. It will allow you to regain confidence in your relationship and restore your interest in your partner and your relationship.

Of course, the other alternative is always that you have genuinely lost interest in your partner and your relationship and does not have a desire to get it back.

Although that is not likely the case, especially since you are reading a book about how to make your relationship work, do not dismiss it as an explanation for what is taking place. If you are losing interest or have lost interest in your long-distance relationship, you will know it. It is not something that you will need to second guess or debate. Your actions and feelings will dictate it for you. Soon enough you will find that your interest runs in other directions. If the issue is much more in-depth such as you no longer love your partner or that your partner has changed for the worse, address these sensitive issues promptly. If you no longer wish to be with them, make them aware of these feelings and decide whether you will walk away from the relationship. If there is a chance of regaining interest, explore it but if not, move on.

If there is one thing that I have learned it is that it does not matter how much you have invested in a long-distance relationship, if the relationship is not right for you or if the person you are with is not right for you, you must walk away from them and never look back. This thought will frighten you, but it is better to do this from right now because you do not want to live with someone and you cannot have a good relationship together. Evaluate your relationship now to figure out the actual reason behind why you may have lost interest.

– Keeping the romance alive –

It is crucial that you make a conscious effort daily to maintain a constant flow of love and appreciation in your relationship. No matter how many times you run out of things to talk about with your partner you can never run out of ways to tell them that you love them. A constant show of affection will reinforce positive feelings in your relationship and ensure that you and your partner think happy thoughts about each other and your relationship.

It is always easy to get angry and to have disagreements every day and multiple times for the day. If you are continually replenishing love in your relationship daily, it hardly leaves room for any negative energy to take precedence over your relationship. Arguments and disagreements are inevitable, but a flow of positive vibrations in your relationship will always alleviate some of the negative things that pour itself into your relationship and allow your relationship to have a better outcome.

Keep the romance alive in your relationship by continually reaffirming your commitment to your partner. Engage in mind, body, and soul arousing conversations that stimulate your senses and brings you to a state in which you are open and honest with your partner. Let this state move you to show your partner how much you are into them and how much you are willing to invest in them. Always make a conscious effort to connect with your partner and be an active part of their day to day lives as much as you can. Get involved in what they do day in and day out. Do this in a way that allows you to relate to them, without making them feel as if you are trying to cling too heavily.

Another way of keeping the romance alive in your

relationship includes sending meaningful messages every day like the notorious morning texts that tell your partner of all the ways you are happy they are still in your life. Be creative. Send gifts to their home or to their place of work to make them feel as special as they are to you.

I like to go big or go home and so my favorite way of keeping the romance alive in my long-distance relationship is to arrive at my partner's doorstep unannounced. I like the thrill that I get from hopping on a plane in a split-second decision. I could be talking to my partner, and in another moment, I get the idea, based off something that he said, to get on a plane and surprise him. It is the boldest choice, but it is also the sweetest and most romantic choice. You, of course, want to be sure that it would be acceptable for you to pop up on your partner.

I do not recommend a pop up in a new long-distance relationship. You have never met face to face, and so this approach may be slightly invasive of your partner's personal life and their space if they did not specifically invite you. It is best to have a strategic plan for when and how you will see each other for the first time in a new long-distance relationship. It allows you to have a proper introduction to your partner's life and their personal space. If, however, you are a couple that has been through these stages, this choice is the most ideal for your mature relationship and the surest way to reinforce the romance between you and your partner. Moreover, of course, there is the sex.

– Seeing each other –

It is essential that you try your best to have face to face or in this case, screen to screen time with your partner. Yes, the old skype video calling! Of course, we have gotten all fancy nowadays with modern technologies that afford us multiple savvy platforms to connect with our long-distance partner face to face. Phone applications such as face time and Whats app video call gives us the convenience of having our beloved at our fingertips – literally. Utilize these platforms to connect with your partner face to face. There is no required amount of time that you need to spend doing this. It depends on your need and your partner's need for interaction. I have been in a long-distance relationship in which I rarely ever used video calling and one in which I lived and breathed video calling. It all depends on your need for this kind of interaction. No one cap fits all.

There are many benefits that you get from persistent screen time with your partner. It helps you to connect more in-depth with the type of person they are. You get to form an opinion of them based on whether their actions complement what they say. You will feel connected to who they are by the movement of their lips as they speak. You will answer questions such as do they smile when they talk, or do they exude seriousness? Is there calmness in their demeanor? What gestures do they perform when they speak? Do they walk around or eat while talking? Is there a particular action that goes with their speech when they are happy or when they are sad? When they lie? These are all things that you would pick up about your partner if you saw each other physically every day. You make up for the lack of physical presence by substituting it for a digital version of face to face interaction in which you can pick up these same traits in your partner as well as if you were both in the same physical space.

If you do not regularly partake in video conferencing in your relationship, I challenge you to begin to do so today. Start small by doing it occasionally until you become accustomed to doing it. As you start to see a positive impact on your relationship, begin to increase the number of times you partake in it until it becomes a part of your usual routine in your relationship. If for some odd reason you do not find video conferencing useful, you may continue to pass on it but be sure not to neglect the usefulness of this tool as it could move your relationship forward to the next step.

If video calling works for you, once you and your partner have gotten into the swing of it, aim to call each other once or twice daily. Use the camera to experiment with different things in your relationship and to share your experiences with your partner. For example, if you routinely go to the hair salon or the barber, take your camera with you and have your partner follow you to these places via the camera. Introduce your partner to the people in your surroundings just as how you would if you were both in the same place together. Continue to experiment this way. Carry your partner along with you for your trips to the doctor's office, the supermarket, the gym, and every other place that you go or things that you do. It will allow your partner to become familiar with how you live your life and enable them to aspire to be where you are and to share your life with you.

– Involve other people whom you can talk to –

One of the best advice that I can give you is to ensure that you are very well socialized when you are in a long-distance relationship. It cannot merely be just you and your partner. For the sake of your sanity, you must allow the company of friends, family, or coworkers. It is unhealthy for you to shut yourself off to the world for the sake of focusing on your relationship. In fact, forsaking social interactions to spend more time to hang around your partner will more than likely hurt your relationship. Everyone needs time to themselves at one point or the other. You need your space, and your partner needs their space. You cannot and should not expect always to bring all your worries and troubles into your relationship. You need to have people in your life that you can be around and hold robust conversations.

You need people in your life that will allow you to give the required space in your relationship. Take a day to treat yourself and a friend to a spa day. Have a designated day out of the week every week that you will dedicate to this. On this day every week communication with your partner is at a minimum. You will maintain contact with them, but they will not be the highlight of your day on this specific day every week.

This time is good for the health of your relationship, and for your psychological health. Doing this on a weekly basis will train you to take control of your personal life. It will remind you of who you are as an individual and teach you to maintain your personality and interests aside from your relationship.

As you continue to do this routinely every week, the day you choose will become a much-anticipated day. It will drive healthy emotions into your relationship while bringing you closer to your partner. Be consistent in dedicating this day to yourself. The element of missing each other will continue to be at work in your relationship in the meantime, creating the perfect amount of desire between you and your partner. Capitalize on this. Use this need to improve other aspects of your relationship.

There are always multiple rewards to reap when you do something exceptional for your relationship. However, keep in mind that it is when you do extraordinary things for yourself first, that your actions can be most impactful. Get in the habit of creating a social life for yourself. When you create this social outlet, use it to occupy yourself and allow a healthy amount of space in your relationship.

– Get busy in your life –

Stay busy in your life. Do things on a regular basis that allows you to have separate time away from your partner. Even though you only see your partner through a screen, it still becomes burdensome to your relationship if you and your partner always pour everything into your relationship. Think about how pollution happens in the environment. It is the same way you can pollute your relationship by dumping any and everything on it all at once. It causes your relationship to experience other issues that are unnecessary and a complete waste of time and good energy.

As attractive as the temptation may be, you should not consume yourself with your relationship; even a long-distance one. A relationship begins to stifle when adequate space does not exist in the relationship for both partners to explore who they are outside of their relationship.

It may be difficult to imagine how you could suffocate when in a long-distance relationship. It happens when you begin to obsess over everything that happens in your relationship and freak out because you are not feeling your relationship on a particular day. It is also when your partner does not send a good morning text or text multiple times for the day, and it becomes an extreme bother to you. When your relationship begins to alter or affect your emotional space in this way, it is a sign that you have become too overwhelmed in your relationship and you need adequate social distractions to help you manage your time.

Go out into the world and do things. Participate in activities of enrichment for your mind and your body. Make a conscious effort to interact with different and exciting people daily and create interesting and exciting experiences. You will notice that as you are becoming more comfortable with your outside surroundings, you will always find positive things that you will come back to your relationship and share with your partner. The more happiness and excitement that you pour into your relationship, the better chances you have of pulling through the time of separation.

Long distance relationships need happiness. It is how they thrive. Couples in regular relationships get to see each other every day or every few days, and so they are constantly resolving the issues that come up in their relationship daily. They are always physically together, and so they are more likely to find different and unique ways to resolve their issues. In a long-distance relationship, you do not have the advantage of seeing each other every day, and so it is crucial that you work extra hard to pour happiness and positivity into your relationship.

***

If you are busy planning for your future with your partner, there will not be a gap in your communication with each other. Your interactions with them will move from one day to the next carried by excitement and appreciation. On those days when you cannot find enthusiasm and gratitude in your relationship, go out into the world, and find inspiration that you will use to fill your relationship with excitement and happiness. Always keep your partner and your relationship as number one priority in everything that you do and in every new experience that you meet. Do this for the enrichment of your wellbeing as well as for the growth of your relationship.

At some point in every relationship, there is a need for some level of adventure. It is ok for you to miss your partner or for your partner to miss you. A healthy amount of desire is always good to have between long-distance couples because it helps them to appreciate each other more in the periods of absence. It is a wise idea for couples to have their separate identities outside of who they are when they are with each other. Showing your partner different sides of who you are as an individual, gives them a sense of enlightenment and adventure and brings out new and exciting aspects of your relationship. The more you engage in activities for individual growth, the more of you there will be to share with your partner. If you are continually figuring out new and impressive things about yourself, it keeps your partner on their toes and allows them to find new ways to appreciate who you are.

– Reflection –

If you find yourself in a position in your relationship where you cannot find anything to talk about on some days, it is ok. If this break from each other cause you to have concerns about losing interest, begin to evaluate your relationship to see whether this is a natural state in your relationship. If the feeling is constant, it is natural. Work on this with your partner at once.

A healthy amount of space is recommended in every relationship no matter what kind. Both you and your partner should want for it and use it to build on your personal growth. You cannot love or care for another person if you do not love and care for yourself first.

So. Breathe. Worrying or growing frantic over every aspect of your relationship will not make the days go faster. Do not spend too much time worrying about what the next day of your relationship will entail. In fact, do not think too hard even about what you and your spouse will talk about for the rest of the current day. Just allow things to flow in your relationship. Let go of your undying need to control every aspect of your relationship even though your intentions may be good. It is a common symptom of long-distance relationships to worry. We worry about when and if we will see our beloved again and if we are not worried about that, we are concerned about micromanaging every little detail of our relationship. We do this out of fear that our relationship has changed, or we constantly obsess over the likelihood that something could possibly go wrong. Shake this urge little by little each day. Inhale. Exhale.

DAY TO DAY:

Worksheet

I stir conflict in my relationship when I am bored:

Your Answer:	Ask Partner:	Total	Total
You:	Partner:	Yes:	No:
YES | NO	YES | NO		

I like to keep my partner alert by playing mind games:

Your Answer:	Ask Partner:	Total	Total
You:	Partner:	Yes:	No:
YES | NO	YES | NO		

I struggle to find things to say to my partner daily:

Your Answer:	Ask Partner:	Total	Total
You:	Partner:	Yes:	No:
YES | NO	YES | NO		

I struggle to keep the romance alive in my relationship:

Your Answer:	Ask Partner:	Total	Total
You:	Partner:	Yes:	No:
YES | NO	YES | NO		

I am losing interest in my relationship:

Your Answer:	Ask Partner:	Total	Total
You:	Partner:	Yes:	No:
YES | NO	YES | NO		

I talk to my partner at least once per day:

Your Answer:	Ask Partner:	Total	Total
You:	Partner:	Yes:	No:
YES | NO	YES | NO		

I constantly plan for the events of my relationship:

Your Answer:	Ask Partner:	Total	Total
You:	Partner:	Yes:	No:
YES | NO	YES | NO		

I show authenticity in my efforts to connect with my partner daily:

Your Answer:	Ask Partner:	Total	Total
You:	Partner:	Yes:	No:
YES | NO	YES | NO		

I see a future for my relationship:

Your Answer:	Ask Partner:	Total	Total
You:	Partner:	Yes:	No:
YES | NO	YES | NO		

Answer Guide:

YES	NO
4	5

Notes:

6
– CONFLICT/ARGUMENTS –

It does not matter what side of an argument you started on or are on currently, if you are both still active in a relationship, one of you must break the ice. Pride has no dwelling in a long-distance relationship. The odds are already against you, and the very last thing you must concern yourself with is pride. Conflict is a natural part of every relationship and in some instances can even be good for a relationship. Conflict can be constructive or destructive. A constructive conflict or argument is the kind that transports you to a positive conclusion in your relationship. It is the moment when you finally under-stand what is causing friction in your relationship. You can resolve conflict faster in your relationship when you can see beyond your perspective and consider the view of your partner. The relationship can take a turn for the better, and healing can occur. A destructive conflict or argument does precisely that – destroy. It destroys your self-worth, your dignity, your level of respect for your-self and your partner, your beliefs about your relationship, and then finally it ruins your relationship.

In normal relationships, couples are more likely to be familiar with the habit of leaving conflict unresolved. Unfortunately, in a long-distance relationship, you cannot afford to display this kind of nonchalant behavior towards your relationship. Regular relationships have a more immediate way of working issues out, and so even in the case of unwillingness and pride, these relationships are always more likely to resolve more problems than a long-distance relationship would. In a long-distance relationship, you and your partner are away from each other, and so if you are unwilling and allow pride to take precedence, your relationship will dissolve.

You must develop a radical approach to resolving conflict in your life and your relationship. When you have a conflict or an argument in your long-distance relationship, it must start and end on the very same day. Your tolerance of conflict in your relationship should be at a minimal. Build up resentment towards it. Condition yourself to reject it.

Conditioning is not hard to do, but it takes time and much determination on your part. Conditioning will allow you to resolve conflict, but it should not replace the complete process of conflict management in your relationship. Note that conflicts and issues are two separate things. Conflict include things such as arguments and disagreements, while issues are prolonged and deep-rooted. A reoccurring conflict can cause issues in your relationship, and unaddressed issues will always stir conflict in your relationship.

Arguments are a conflict that may either be a part of a more significant issue or about something that genuinely came up at the specific point in time when the argument occurred. Even if the argument is about something at the particular moment, the driving forces behind the debate have a deeper connection to a more significant issue in the relationship. To stop the reoccurrence of conflict in your relationship due to underlying issues, you must find what the deep-rooted problem is in the relationship.

The best way to approach this is to talk it out with your partner. Approach your partner calmly and set aside a time when both of you can give your undivided attention to each other. Speak in a low, relaxed voice as you engage your partner in a meaningful conversation about what is taking place in the relationship. The method of communication that you will use is dependent on the details of the reoccurring conflict. For instance, if arguments usually start due to a particular look or facial expression, do not use video calling to address this issue for the first time. It will only create a distraction and make the situation a lot worse than it was before you made the call.

Choose your mode of communication wisely. When couples continuously use ineffective communication methods to solve a conflict, it causes frustration to the point where some couples end their relationship. It becomes hard for them to imagine a resolve and so they decide that giving up is their best alternative. When you are addressing the issues, advocate for a change in the method of communication used. Try talking on the phone if video calling is an issue. If you cannot speak calmly, try texting or use voice messaging. This way, you can listen to the tone of your message before sending it.

Over the years I have become very fond of the free calling application, Whats App. Whats App is a platform on which you can call, text or video call anyone in the world if they have a data connection. You may have heard of it. Whats app is a cell phone application that lets you know when your recipient receives and reads your messages. A clock means that your message is waiting for a data connection to transfer to your recipient. One clear check mark means your message was sent but is awaiting transmission to your recipient's phone. This check mark could signify that their phone is either turned off or does not have a data connection. It could also mean that they blocked you from being able to send them messages through the application. Two transparent check marks indicate that your recipient has received your message. The recipient has received a notification about the message but has not opened the message. When the two check marks turn blue, that means that your recipient has read your message and the application gives you the exact time when it happens.

Many people use the functionality of this application for all the wrong reasons, but the true benefits of the application can make the difference in connecting you with your partner if used correctly. These features are not a way for you to become obsessive if your partner does not respond to your messages promptly. The main purpose of the platform is to provide a convenient way of connecting with your partner. Of course, if your partner habitually reads your messages and leaves them unanswered, you can certainly draw assumptions from that. If you suspect anything, address it calmly.

The best feature of this application is the ability to delete messages sent to your recipient before they read it. This feature is useful in situations where you have said too many things that you did not mean and that could hurt your relationship. Consider it to practice self-control. Your partner can see when you delete messages, but they are not able to tell what was in the message. I recommend the use of this feature only in situations where you feel it is necessary to avert additional conflict in your relationship.

— Stop talking —

The very first concept that I will introduce to you for resolving conflict in your long-distance relationship is to stop talking. When you find yourself in an intense moment with your partner, stop talking. Nothing else that you say in the situation during a heated argument will cause the argument to go in a positive direction, even if you feel what you are saying is something good. In a forceful discussion, you only hear half of what your partner is saying. You phase out the other half by your prompt responses to the bits and pieces that you heard.

It happens because we always think we know where the conversation is going, rather than listening to find out precisely where. In most instances, you do not know where the discussion is going, and so it is best to allow your partner to complete their thought process and give yourself a moment to respond most adequately.

To begin the recovery process, you must get rid of the communication noise. Communication noise is any influence that interrupts your ability to get a message across to your partner. Getting rid of communication noise becomes much simpler when you start with yourself. If you are going to create real change, it always must begin with you. If you can take control of yourself and remain silent in a moment of ear-piercing noise, you will find that you will hear more of the essential things that your partner has to say. The bigger picture that will guide you to the issues in your relationship is in what your partner is saying. It is not a question that outside factors and distractions will attempt to make a substantial impact on your relationship. These external factors are meant to test your relationship. Therefore, it is essential for you to learn how to cancel the noise in your relationship and allow effective communication to take superiority in resolving issues in your relationship.

– Admit your role –

In your relationship, there is no impartial party in an argument. If you were a part of the conversation, you are also wrong. If not for the sake of anything else, take responsibility for your actions in the name of peace.

Apologize even if you believe you have done nothing wrong. We prove our strength in those moments when we face persecution but still find it within ourselves to apologize for the part we play, whether we believe our actions are justifiable. That is growth. That is a strength.

What you stand to gain from taking responsibility is much more important than being right. I know very well how it feels to know that you are right and want to claim it. I used to pride myself on being right until I realized that every time I was right and felt that I had defeated my partner, I felt empty inside. Always being right never does anything much for you other than give you the title of always being right. My most significant achievement and highest sense of fulfillment came when I was able to apologize and talk to my partner. I get to remain close to the person that I love, and that reason alone is more than enough to restore peace in my relationship.

The most unfortunate thing about always being right is that it is always lonely. You will end up losing the one you love, and that sacrifice is never worth it. There is much more power in taking responsibility for the role you played. It affords you control over the situation, and it shows that you are strong without using force. An even better advantage of taking responsibility is that you can be confident it will hold the attention of your partner. In an argument, everyone wants to be right. The people in the argument are only arguing because they have an undying need to prove that they are right and that the other person is wrong. It is the energy that arguments run on. If there is no right person and no wrong person, there would be no argument. Therefore, if you take responsibility first, your partner will listen to you because they want the satisfaction of hearing you say that you are wrong. Do not be afraid to take a loss for the sake of your relationship. It is better to be wrong in one situation than to lose the person you love over something that is irrelevant to your relationship.

When you take responsibility for your role, this triggers a feeling of repentance in your partner instantaneously. That is the beauty of taking responsibility. It is contagious, and it dispenses good energy throughout the entire situation. It makes everything better for you and for resolving conflict in your relationship. Once this exchange happens, you and your partner will begin to have good feelings about each other again. Over time, this will bring you closer together in a stronger bond than ever before. When two people who love each other can move past conflict, there is a natural outpouring of good vibrations that causes them to become inspired by each other. Once you and your partner fully resolve the issues in your relationship, you will discover a new appreciation for each other. You both will appreciate and admire the level of growth that you see in each other. You will both now feel that you can maintain a stable level of respect, communication, and problem-solving skills to sustain your relationship.

– Drop it –

When you and your partner close a conflict or finds a resolution to an issue and are in a satisfying place with a stronger bond, do yourself a huge favor and drop the subject. One of the biggest incapability that kills long-distance relationships is the inability to let things go. Holding on to things is like a growing tumor in your relationship. Once it gets to a certain point, you will not be able to remove it fast enough, before it spreads into more prominent and more damaging problems in your relationship.

Letting go of things is easier said than done and I do not expect that you will now be able to let go of things just because I said so. It is a process that will take some time to adjust to, but you must not exaggerate the time needed to do so. You will not always know that you are holding on to certain things in your relationship. At any point, a subject can resurface, and you find yourself reverting to old issues that have already been addressed and dismissed in your relationship. It instigates a whole new problem in your relationship for the fact that none of the related issues have a genuine and permanent resolve. The frustration from this realization will cause your relationship to begin to dissolve.

In a long-distance relationship, some of the deep-rooted issues stem from outside factors, and then there are also the issues that we create ourselves. Holding grudges, keeping secrets, malice, and never genuinely granting forgiveness, is only a few of how we do so. If you consciously hold on to things in your relationship after finding a resolve, you are single-handedly destroying your relationship. If you hold a grudge against your partner without seriously trying to resolve it, that is like putting a nail in the coffin that will bury your relationship.

The best way to avoid this cycle of unnecessary conflict in your relationship is to learn how to let things go. If you find that you absolutely cannot let something go, it is because you did not get the resolve that you want. You need closure. Find a calm and neutral way of revisiting the unresolved issues. Once you visit these issues and find a new resolve, let it go.

If you decide that the issue is something that you must address because of critical unanswered questions that could affect your relationship, find a way to approach your partner without seeming as if you are trying to repeat old issues. Start by assuring your partner that your intentions are not to reiterate old problems, but that you still need closure in some aspects of what took place.

It is easier to approach your partner about this soon after the original problem. The longer you wait, the harder it will be for you to explain to your partner why you need to revisit those old issues. When you are in discussion with your partner about the problem once again, this time around, you must ensure that you remain active in the conversation and are actively seeking your desired resolution to the issue. This time around it not about your partner. This time is about you getting closure and being able to move forward in your relationship.

CONFLICT/ARGUMENT:

Worksheet

There are unresolved issues in my relationship:

Your Answer:	Ask Partner:	Total	Total
You:	Partner:	Yes:	No:
YES | NO	YES | NO		

There is reoccurring conflict in my relationship:

Your Answer:	Ask Partner:	Total	Total
You:	Partner:	Yes:	No:
YES | NO	YES | NO		

I usually give a prompt response during an argument:

Your Answer:	Ask Partner:	Total	Total
You:	Partner:	Yes:	No:
YES | NO	YES | NO		

It is hard to let go of issues in my relationship:

Your Answer:	Ask Partner:	Total	Total
You:	Partner:	Yes:	No:
YES | NO	YES | NO		

I sometimes hold grudges against my partner without their knowledge:

Your Answer:	Ask Partner:	Total	Total
You:	Partner:	Yes:	No:
YES | NO	YES | NO		

I take responsibility for the part I played in the conflict in my relationship:

Your Answer:	Ask Partner:	Total	Total
You:	Partner:	Yes:	No:
YES | NO	YES | NO		

My partner and I can maintain a stable level of respect, communication, and problem-solving skills to sustain our relationship:

Your Answer:	Ask Partner:	Total	Total
You:	Partner:	Yes:	No:
YES | NO	YES | NO		

I am usually satisfied with the outcome after resolving a conflict in my relationship:

Your Answer:	Ask Partner:	Total	Total
You:	Partner:	Yes:	No:
YES | NO	YES | NO		

Answer Guide:

YES	NO
3	5

Notes:

7
– TRUST –

An interesting thing about trust is how hard it is to earn and how easy it is to lose. Trust is delicate grounds in any relationship and couples try their hardest to avoid doing things that could sever the trust that they have built between them. Sometimes these efforts are successful if worked vigorously, but sometimes we fail miserably and end up hurting ourselves and the people we love the most. Trust is a delicacy. The good thing for all of us long-distance lovers is that trust comes as a part of the initial package when we form a love connection over a distance.

The biggest thing that I have experienced over the years with regards to trust in long-distance relationships is how we trick ourselves into believing that our partner must earn our trust when we have already given them our trust by inviting them into our lives. In a long-distance relationship, trust is not the most significant factor in your relationship that you must work tirelessly to build. When you enter a long-distance relationship and especially the kind that starts from a distance such as online, at the point when you decide to take the relationship to the next level, you also choose to trust your partner. You choose to believe in everything that your partner says, and likewise, they trust everything that you say. Truthfully, you do not have to earn trust in the initial stages of a long-distance relationship; it happens willingly. When the relationship gets to a point where couples must gain their partner's trust, that means that the initial bond of trust is absent.

In these modern times, honesty is a rare treasure in relationships. The surest way to lose your partner's trust is not to tell the entire story of who you are. The emphasis on explaining the full story is because of the complex dynamics of a long-distance relationship. If you are not telling the whole story about who you are, you are actively trying to deceive your partner. Deception is the deadliest sin in a long-distance relationship. Deception of any kind, or of any size can break trust. Deception carries much weight because unlike the other things that you can do to break your partner's trust, deception is worst because it is a conscious decision that you make.

You cannot accidentally deceive someone. Deception comes from knowing a weakness that the target displays. This weakness is what makes the deceiver believe that they are an excellent target. When trust breaks in this way it is near impossible to get it back. Always choose to be honest with your partner. It is easy to lie to your partner when you are in a long-distance relationship, but you must resist this temptation. Consider the impact that it will have on your partner. Also, consider how breaking that bond of trust will affect you person-ally as well as how it will influence your outlook on life. We tend to focus on our perception of the advantage that we get from deceiving others, and we always forget the hard lessons that it will teach us in the end.

The thing about broken trust that makes it so devastating is the fact that you never know exactly how it will change your life or the life of the person whom you deceive. It is an unnecessary risk that you take. You have nothing to gain and everything to lose regardless of the outcome. As you go through life, you will find that morality is the second biggest teacher in life. It falls second after time. You may not feel the consequences of your actions immediately or even thirty years down the line, but rest assured that the things that you put out in the world have their cunning way of coming back around to you.

– Forming Trust –

Trust matriculates in a relationship when words match with actions. What you say must correlate with what you do. That proves to your partner that you are an honest person. It is at the point of proving to be honest, and pure at heart that you gain the trust of your partner. Since the factor of seeing action is absent in a long-distance relationship, you must put significant effort into holding your partner accountable for the things that they say. That allows you to know if they are consistent.

Indeed, it will be challenging to try to keep up with everything that your partner says. The trick is to not focus too much on remembering every detail but to form a complete opinion of your partner based on what they say and what they do. Think about things that your partner says and do and conceptualize them. Use this to form your perception of who they are. If you continue to do this, you will know if there is inconsistency in whom they proclaim to be.

– Maintain Trust –

After forming trust in your long-distance relationship, the next phase is to maintain mutual trust throughout your relationship. You do this by effectively managing conflict in your relationship, by remaining open in your relationship, and by making a conscious decision to stay honest in everything that you say and do in your relationship.

If you are in a long-distance relationship and your partner continuously use phrases such as, "you must gain my trust" or "for me to trust you" then your relationship does not have mutual trust. It poses a problem for you especially if you already invested trust in the relationship. This one-sided trust becomes burdensome to the relationship and causes conflict in your relationship.

This type of situation stems from our constant need to have perfection in our long-distance relationship. Unbelievably, many people in long-distance relationships swear that if they are going to put themselves through the agony and frustration that comes with being in a long-distance relationship, they must find the perfect partner worth the sacrifice. As a result, they begin to hold the mere human that they are dating to ridiculously ambitious standards that they cannot meet. In many ways, they set up their partner for failure and string them along on a journey to earn their trust when they know very well their partner will never be worthy.

If you remain open and truthful in your relationship, it should not have to be like pulling teeth to maintain trust in the relationship. Say what you mean and mean what you say. Always hold yourself to a high standard of consistency. Make it your number one priority. Show your partner all the effort that you make to ensure that you are always constant and always deliver on the promises that you make.

Be realistic. Do not set expectations in your relationship that you cannot follow. It is one of the fastest ways to lose trust in your relationship. Security is vital in every relationship and even more so in long-distance relationships. Being in a long-distance relationship means that you must always prove yourself to your partner. In a regular relationship, this would be exhausting since ordinary couples see each other every day. However, in a long-distance relationship we need constant interaction and so proving yourself becomes the most exciting part of the relationship. In a long-distance relationship, we invent new and exciting ways to remind our partner that we love them. Doing this helps us to maintain an intimate bond with them. Appreciate the importance of always following through on the expectations that you create in your relationship. Do not entertain mediocrity in your relationship by making promises and then discarding them. Your partner will not take you seriously, and your relationship will never get to the point where it can grow into a future.

The good news about lost trust is that you can always restore it. The bad news is that it is near impossible to do so. People who usually say once trust is out the door you can never get it back are not telling the whole truth. You can always regain trust, but that decision is not up to you to make. This decision is for the partner that is on the receiving end of the deception. Nine times out of ten, that person is not interested. If you are genuinely remorseful for what you did to lose their trust, you must accept that you will need to start from square one to have even the slightest chance of redemption.

Start by approaching their heart. When you lose someone's trust, you do not regain it by aiming for trust - you already lost it. Start by unlocking the door that leads to their innermost being – the heart. That is where you will find the way back to their good graces and even earn back their trust. To reach their core, all you must do on your part is to be genuine. Learn from all the mistakes that you made previously and make a calculated effort to prove yourself worthy of their trust. This process could be simple for you, or it could be the hardest thing you ever do in your entire life. Never give up. Decide whether the trust of your partner is worth the fight. This process is hard and painful. It will seem as if you are getting nowhere. It will go on for days, months or even years before your partner trusts you again or before you decide to give up. One of the two will happen with time.

– Roadblock –

Roadblocks are common in relationships when trust is out the door. Yes, there are many other ways that you may experience a barrier in your relationship, but trust is the most critical. If there is anything left of your relationship, you should always try to salvage it. Things will inescapably get harder in your relationship, but you must go through the changes of growth to move your relationship from one stage to the next. If you are in this situation right now and you and your partner are still active in your relationship, that means that you are both willing to do what is necessary to get back to a place of mutual trust in your relationship. That is good.

Do not lose sight of this. You and your partner must equally contribute to rebuilding your relationship no matter who deceived who and for what reason. Be very observant of this. You both must decide to work on your relationship. Even if you were the one who lost the trust of your partner, your partner must work with you wholeheartedly to fix the issues. They must decide to be all in or choose to walk away. I do not know about you, but I have always valued the concept of time, and I would hate to waste time on a relationship that ended weeks, months, or years before anyone realized it. It happens many times in long-distance relationships. Distance allows ample time for people to reevaluate their desires based on changes that they experience in their lives, and so many people take decisions regardless of how their partner will react.

The distance makes it exceptionally easier for long-distance relationships to dissolve over time when there is an ongoing conflict. It is easy to shut your partner out when you are far away from each other. You do not see them, and this makes it possible to walk away with the least emotional impact. It may also be a comfort to know that there is no chance that you will run into them or ever see them again. For some, this is good news.

Do not panic. Trust is a delicate topic in long-distance relationships. Broken trust can decide the faith of your relationship but rest assured that unwillingness to cope and lack of commitment, destroys more long-distance relationships than lack of trust ever has. You can work on rebuilding trust in your relationship if you and your partner are willing to do the hard work. A long-distance relationship will always require the same amount of maintenance, the same amount of effort, and the same amount of conflict resolution as any other relationship. You do not get an easy pass because of the distance. In fact, the distance makes it even harder.

Take your time. If your relationship is going to mend it must mend on its own time with continuous work by you and your partner. Do not rush to get back to a manufactured place of happiness. Take your time with the changes and embrace them. Decide to enjoy each other and enjoy the satisfaction that you feel in the moment. You will feel incredibly grateful that your relationship has another chance to grow. Live in these moments. These moments will strike your hearts and inspire the love between you and your partner. This level of mutual embrace will invite trust back into your relationship.

Be sincere. If you can be purely open and brutally honest with yourself about who you are your relationship can have support to build a future. Decide to be honest. It is that simple. Honesty is as much of choice as brushing your teeth or changing your underwear. Honesty is simple, and it affords you happiness if you can be consistent. Have faith in your partner's ability to see you for who you are through your honesty. Learn to give your partner time to heal and to learn how to trust you on their own time. In the meantime, cultivate an atmosphere that communication in your relationship remains open and flowing constantly. If you are going to build trust, you both must feel safe and secure in your relationship and can effortlessly approach each other to resolve issues positively and productively. Always be willing to take responsibility for any part that you play and make a sincere effort to right the wrongs in your relationship.

Be proactive. Create an atmosphere that continuously opens more room for trust in your relationship. Do not sit blindly and wait for trust to fall back into your relationship. Get up and do something. Keep the wheels of trust turning in your relationship by inspiring each other daily. Create a safe place in each other where you can both practice how to have faith in your ability to respect and do right by each other. When you begin to practice faithfulness in your relationship, this opens the door to trust. Be deliberate in your efforts to bring trust back into your relationship. Listen to the needs of your partner and follow them carefully. Take careful steps to reassure your partner of your worthiness of their trust and of your commitment to growing your relationship to the next level.

TRUST:

Worksheet

It is easy to lie to my partner:

Your Answer:	Ask Partner:	Total	Total
You:	Partner:	Yes:	No:
YES | NO	YES | NO		

What my partner does not know will not hurt them:

Your Answer:	Ask Partner:	Total	Total
You:	Partner:	Yes:	No:
YES | NO	YES | NO		

My partner will never be worthy of my trust:

Your Answer:	Ask Partner:	Total	Total
You:	Partner:	Yes:	No:
YES | NO	YES | NO		

I make promises in my relationship, but I rarely keep them:

Your Answer:	Ask Partner:	Total	Total
You:	Partner:	Yes:	No:
YES | NO	YES | NO		

I set unattainable expectations in my relationship:

Your Answer:	Ask Partner:	Total	Total
You:	Partner:	Yes:	No:
YES | NO	YES | NO		

My partner knows all vital details about who I am:

Your Answer:	Ask Partner:	Total	Total
You:	Partner:	Yes:	No:
YES | NO	YES | NO		

My actions match my word:

Your Answer:	Ask Partner:	Total	Total
You:	Partner:	Yes:	No:
YES | NO	YES | NO		

My partner is an honest person:

Your Answer:	Ask Partner:	Total	Total
You:	Partner:	Yes:	No:
YES | NO	YES | NO		

My relationship has mutual trust:

Your Answer:	Ask Partner:	Total	Total

You:	Partner:	Yes:	No:
YES | NO	YES | NO		

Answer Guide:

YES	NO
4	5

Notes:

8
– SOCIAL MEDIA –

Social media is like that big elephant in the room that people in a long-distance relationship tiptoe around frequently in order to avoid confrontation. It starts with the expectation to announce the relationship publicly to acknowledge the validity of the relationship to friends, family, and personal and professional acquaintances. What usually ends up happening is somewhere along the line, being on social media as a couple becomes the most significant deciding factor in how the relationship dynamics changes. Social media has evolved into a powerful platform and the lines between personal and professional cross on a frequent basis with devastating ends. People either do not recognize boundaries, or they do not care for them.

The most significant rule in being on social media as a couple is that you must never exaggerate or try too hard to validate your relationship on social media. The moment you decide to do this is the moment when things will begin to go wrong in your relationship. Subtlety remains the best course of action in communicating the status of your relationship on a public platform. It is so for personal reasons as well as to maintain professional identities.

Approach social media with delicacy at all times. Before you indulge in posting on any social media platform about your relationship, think about the outcomes of your actions. The result can be positive if you are confident that your relationship is healthy and growing healthier in private; however, the effect can be extremely devasting if your relationship begins to wither publicly on social media. Think carefully through the different possible consequences. By doing this, you can make an informed decision about posting on social media.

You are thinking to yourself that a topic such as social media should not be so complicated and in fact, it is the topics like social media, which are neglected in our long-distance relationships, that always comes back around to haunt us. Social media is one of those simple things that should not be as complicated as it is in our lives. However, due to its growing impact in the world that we live in, it becomes the center of our lives in a long-distance relationship. Social media has a constant love-hate relationship amongst long-distance couples. We love it because it keeps us connected to each other in many ways, but we also hate it because its impact can grow wildly and kill our relationship. The key to preventing this from happening is to always reflect on your use of social media platforms as it relates to your partner. Have an open line of communication about social media in your relationship to prevent surprises.

– Posting on social media –

Posting about your relationship on social media is not the most critical aspect of your relationship. It does not add anything to your relationship, but it takes a lot if it wants to. It is reasonable why anyone would want their partner to acknowledge them on social media, and it is necessary for your partner to do so depending on their social affiliation with social media. If your partner is someone who does not frequently use social media or does not use social media at all – like they do not even have a Facebook page – it is not necessary to force them to create a social media presence for the sake of the relationship. Changing their relationship status to, "in a relationship," and tagging you as the person they are in a relationship with is not an urgent issue. All of this is not necessary if you and your partner had not been using social media habitually before your relationship. It does not need to happen by force.

My stance on social media will always be that it is not necessary to force yourself to post just because you feel compelled to do it. If you and your partner are frequently interacting with social media, then it is a given that both of you should naturally want to say something now and then to acknowledge each other. If both of you are on social media every day and you bypass each other; never tagging, commenting, or sharing a picture then something is not right in the relationship. This type of behavior is not natural. Unless of course, there is a prior agreement that there will be no publicity in the relationship. If no such deal is in place, yet your partner seems reluctant to share news of your relationship, something is taking place in your relationship, and you should be curious to find out what it is.

The social media game is a very tricky game. I may have my reservations about oversharing on social media, but I am confident that lack of sharing on social media, under these circumstances, is a huge red flag – if not the biggest one – in a long-distance relationship. If you evaluate your relationship and you find that your partner does not have a substantial reason for why they have not shared you on social media be direct and ask them. If your partner becomes reluctant or suspicious of the reason as to why you are requesting, explain your reasoning to them and remain focus on getting the specific answers that you seek. One thing you should never allow to happen in your long-distance relationship is to let a reluctant partner cause you to feel as if you are overreacting over social media because more than likely, you are not.

Social media is significant in our lives in a long-distance relationship. It always baffles me when people pretend as if nothing can happen over the internet. After marrying a man that I met through an online dating website; and for the millions of other people falling in love all over the internet, I can tell you for a fact that a lot of unexpected things happens through social media. People fall in love, fall out of love, get married, and divorced. It all happens through social media daily. If you feel in your gut that something is not right about your partner's social media conduct towards you, initiate a conversation to discourse the matter.

– Acknowledgment –

Acknowledgment is about introducing your long-distance partner to your social circle. The same way you would not personally invite a date to an event and not acknowledge that they are there is the same way you do not invite your partner to your social media pages and act as if you do not know each other. Acknowledgment has less to do with social media as a platform and more to do with social media as a commonplace to unite family and friends and the things that are most important in those relationships.

In the modern world, we share everything on social media. If we are eating, we feel compelled to snap a picture of our food and post it to our social media page before we even begin to bite. Some people also wait for likes before they even touch the food. Wherever we go and whatever we do, we prioritize to share information about ourselves on social media, not because we are bored, but because it is how our family and friends can watch us grow and to continually know about what we are doing in our everyday lives. Truthfully, without social media, many friendships would end, and many family members would fall out of touch with each other. We cannot deny the usefulness of the platform or the statements that we make when we use it.

If you frequently or even occasionally indulge in social media, you make the statement that the platform is of importance to you in sharing certain aspects of your life. If you are in a long-distance relationship, your relationship becomes an aspect of your life and therefore will expect your acknowledgment on social media as well. When you fail to engage them, it sends a very straightforward message to your partner. It is your responsibility to ensure that you communicate well with your partner your reasons for not acknowledging your relationship; likewise, your partner must relate to you their intentions if they have not done so either.

The best way to go about social media acknowledgment and not end up in hot water over it is to be completely honest with your partner. If your partner is someone who indulges in social media, but you do not, you would have known this from the beginning of the relationship. That is an ideal time to let your stance on the topic be known to your partner.

If you do not want to post on social media about your relationship, there is no need to go around the issue and try to hide it. Be completely open and honest in telling your partner about why you do not feel it is best for you to post about them on a public platform. Once the atmosphere in the relationship is open where honesty can thrive, always choose to be honest with each other. If you both can accept what each has to offer in reasoning, then there is no point in prolonging the issue, and you can move on from the subject.

– Social media conduct –

If not for anyone else, you owe it to yourself to not

embarrass yourself on social media. Do not confront anyone on social media about your partner or your relationship. In a long-distance relationship, there is not much to go by to judge the faithfulness of our partner and to fill that void some people tend to turn their attention to social media for answers. I will not say that this is a small idea because many couples are guilty of cheating on their partners on social media. What I will call it instead is an active waste of energy and a disaster waiting to happen.

If you are trying to figure out if your long-distance partner is faithful and social media is your only way of finding this, your relationship is already in trouble. The only right way of figuring out whether you have a faithful long-distance partner is to have a solid idea of who they are as an individual. When you have a good idea of who your partner is, you can apply common sense to figure out whether or not they are faithful. Many of us already know that we have an unfaithful partner before we go searching for "solid" proof. If you are scoping social media with the intent to catch your partner doing something they are not supposed to be doing, chances are you already know that they are doing things that they are not supposed to. Therefore, if you search and you find something on social media that suggests that your partner may be unfaithful to you, do not lure attention to yourself by destroying your dignity and embarrassing yourself publicly.

Always be conscious of how you represent yourself on social media. A lot of the times people are of the belief that social media is for personal and social use and that any behavior is acceptable. They believe it is confidential information and that they can control whom they allow to see it. It may have been so around twenty or so years ago, but in today's modern world your social media pages represent your personal and professional brand, and you have no control over where it will end up in the world.

The use of social media for personal reasons is almost obsolete. Social media is now mostly about transacting business and maintaining a professional portfolio. Therefore, it is crucial that you filter your activities and the verbiage that you use on these platforms. The negative things that you are impelling to write on social media now, and may very well feel righteous in doing, will be the very same things that you will regret in the future when you finally see the adverse impact that it has on your professional and personal life. Once you put something out in the internet world, you lose control of it. You no longer control where it goes or who sees it, and as a lover of all things screenshots, I can tell you for a fact that you will eventually regret doing it.

Another thing that I will caution you from doing is blocking your partner on social media. Do not use this platform to start a war in your relationship. If you do not want your partner on your social media, do not add them there in the first place. If you add them but no longer wish to have them there, let them know that you will remove them and be prepared to provide a good reason as to why. Once you add your partner on social media, if you are still in a relationship, there is not a good enough reason that will suffice as to why you want to change your mind about having your partner in your social circle. It sends a huge statement to your partner and to everyone on your social media who knows of your relationship. It will draw unnecessary attention to yourself and attract a lot of unimportant people who will ask you a series of irrelevant questions about your relationship. The same goes for blocking your partner via text messaging or calling. Take my advice and never prevent your partner from having clear communication with you. It brings a whole host of negative vibe into your relationship, and it does not benefit you in any way.

– Sliding in the DMs –

One of the biggest things we want to know about our long-distance partner as it relates to social media is if anything is "going down in the DMs." If you are not familiar with this modern phrase, it simply means that many love interests are pouring into your partner on their social media pages through direct messaging or "DM" for short. Before you seek the answer to this question, however, I want to challenge you to think about what is going down in your DM. What do your direct messages look like across your social media pages?

If you are wondering how your inbox tells you what is going on in your partner's inbox, the answer is it does not. What you are doing by thinking about your inbox is to ensure that you have cleared yourself of any hypocritical intent. A lot of times couples argue over who is talking to who or who is flirting with who on social media and it usually ends with one partner justifying their actions and finding reasons why the other person is wrong. If you believe that the people whom you converse with in your direct message are "innocent flirting," "fling," or "doesn't mean anything," you cannot seriously inquire about what your partner is doing, unless you are willing to accept that they might give you the very same answer, whether it is the truth or they are lying.

Suppose you are genuinely innocently conversing? The answer is it does not matter. It is like being in a court of law; you cannot change a law to implicate the other party while vindicating yourself for the same crime on the grounds of a technically. If you are both conversing in your direct messages, you are both doing something that you are not supposed to be doing.

How will either of you find out if no one goes snooping? The answer is you do not. This information has a particularly clever way of finding us at the right time when the information is most useful to us.

There may also be a second and third option for you in this matter. Through option two, you can decide to omit social media as a method that would be suspicious of as a way for your partner to be unfaithful. If you go with option two, it could mean that you are either in denial or that things are going down in your DMs. Through option three, you decide that you will not accept any form of social media contact with other people as acceptable from your partner. In this case, you also solemnly swear you will never conduct yourself in the same manner. If you go with option three, it is likely that you are highly insecure and loves conflict, or you are entirely unaware of the impact that taking a decision such as this will have on your relationship.

Of course, there is secret option number four. Option four would be for you and your partner to build a trust-filled and respectable relationship together where you both can equally acknowledge each other in the presence of your family, friends, and professional networks on social media. If something suspicious were to come across your social media page or direct message, through option four, you would both work matters out tenderly, privately, and respectfully as a couple. It is up to you and your partner to decide whether there will be an option four. It is an agreement between both of you to grow your relationship effectively in a positive way. The basic idea behind filtering your social media presence in reaction to your relationship is a precaution to save yourself a whole ton of unnecessary conflict, arguments, and mistrust.

SOCIAL MEDIA:

Worksheet

My partner and I have a clear understanding of our use of social media concerning our relationship:

Your Answer:	Ask Partner:	Total	Total
You:	Partner:	Yes:	No:
YES | NO	YES | NO		

I know my partner very well:

Your Answer:	Ask Partner:	Total	Total
You:	Partner:	Yes:	No:
YES | NO	YES | NO		

I filter my social media presence in relation to my relationship:

Your Answer:	Ask Partner:	Total	Total
You:	Partner:	Yes:	No:
YES | NO	YES | NO		

I get suspicious when my spouse does not post about me on social media:

Your Answer:	Ask Partner:	Total	Total
You:	Partner:	Yes:	No:
YES | NO	YES | NO		

Social media causes conflict in my relationship:

Your Answer:	Ask Partner:	Total	Total
You:	Partner:	Yes:	No:
YES | NO	YES | NO		

There is something suspicious about my partner's social media conduct towards me:

Your Answer:	Ask Partner:	Total	Total
You:	Partner:	Yes:	No:
YES | NO	YES | NO		

I sometimes look to social media for cues on whether my partner is faithful:

Your Answer:	Ask Partner:	Total	Total
You:	Partner:	Yes:	No:
YES | NO	YES | NO		

I sometimes block my partner from my phone or on my social media pages:

Your Answer:	Ask Partner:	Total	Total
You:	Partner:	Yes:	No:
YES | NO	YES | NO		

Answer Guide:

YES	NO
3	5

Notes:

9
– FAMILY –

In the initial stages of a long-distance relationship, you spend the least amount of energy on the thought of family and the significant role that they play in your relationship. Family consists of both your family and your partner's family. Family will always be a factor in a long-distance relationship. It is crucial that you learn how to correctly approach the topic of family, especially in the initial stages of your relationship. Whether you realize it, family plays a significant role in determining if the relationship between you and your partner will work. In a long-distance relationship, your partner's family is the most significant indicator of who your partner truly is and can help you in a major way to put your relationship into perspective.

– None disclosure to family –

The family is usually one of the last topics discussed in

a long-distance relationship. If not done in the right way, there will be tension in the relationship. The introduction to family is a delicate topic. Everyone is simply trying their absolute best to protect their interest. It is tricky to introduce the person you are dating long-distance to the family because of the fear that the relationship will not work out. If you view your long-distance relationship in this context, you will find that you will encounter many difficulties in your relationship.

Another factor is the fear of being embarrassed. Many people in long-distance relationships have a constant fear of being embarrassed about their relationship. It is mostly due to the old standards of long-distance relationships that make this kind of relationship seem extremely silly. It is always a risk to go to family and introduce the concept of a long-distance relationship, especially if the concept has never been considered in the family before. You can never be sure of how family will react, but that is ok. Really. Family does not need to accept your relationship immediately, and you should not expect them to. Your biggest concern in your long-distance relationship is not family. It is your faith and confidence in your relationship. If you have even the slightest doubt about your relationship, you should take caution in approaching family about your relationship. When you are ready to contact family, you must build a compelling case. Prove to them that your relationship has a solid foundation by maintaining a healthy relationship complemented by solid plans for the future of the relationship.

There are still many people who believe that long-distance relationships are meaningless and destined to end badly. This is due to the old idea of long-distance relationships as either a silly idea created by young, foolish people, or a situation that some married couples end up in due to circumstances beyond their control. Unbelievably, there are also many people who are active in a long-distance relationship and swears to keep it a secret, not only from family but period. These long-distance daters are living a double life, and although they enjoy being with their partner, the partner must remain a secret, at least until a plan is underway where they can be together physically. It is usually at this point when these types of long-distance daters decide to reveal their relationship; when there is only a brief period left for them to be apart. To them, their relationship does not come off as silly to the people whom they will tell, mainly family.

I can go out on a limb for another reasoning behind the non-disclosure to family, but I do not think you are going to like it so brace yourself. Whenever you are in a long-distance relationship, an initial introduction to the family, even an informal one, serves as an acknowledgment to the family that someone exists in your life. It usually happens well after a couple of months have passed. Even if it is a hello to a brother or sister, some form of introduction occurs. With bigger fishes such as mom and dad, the acknowledgment of the relationship delays due to the significance of what it means to "meet the parents." Most people also leave their parents for last due to the pressure that accompanies introducing a long-distance relationship. It is no surprise that parents will be suspicious and so it is understandable if your partner decides to leave them for last. Other than parents, everyone else in the immediate family is usually an easier target to break in the news and so as far as extended family is concerned, there is no excuse.

If your partner is dragging their feet on introducing you to their family, this may be the biggest red flag waved yet. In a situation like this, your partner must immediately provide you with a reason for the non-disclosure. If they are unwilling to give you the answers that you seek, pay attention, and proceed accordingly. Do not try to force the information out of your partner, even if you know that the non-disclosure is deliberate. A deliberate non-disclosure to the family could be with or without an ulterior motive, and so it is best to approach the situation calmly and ask the right questions to get to the truth.

***

If you are in any one of these positions, I want you to understand that the old concept of long-distance relationships being pointless, shameful, or otherwise due to inconvenience, is long gone. We live in a time when long-distance relationships make up a considerable amount of the population of people who are in love. People are falling in love at rapid speeds, disregarding all obstacles in their way – even distance.

The subject of the family can be incredibly intimidating, mainly because this phase of the relationship usually tells us the truth about what we will experience in the relationship further down the line. Do not be afraid of what you learn in this phase. Be patient with the process and do not feel discouraged at the first bad turn of events. Expect that situations can go many ways once family is involved. Always remain true to who you are. Never try to be someone else to prove yourself.

– When do I meet the family? –

The decision of when to meet family depends solely on the two people in the relationship. It could happen a week into the relationship or months out. It depends on your comfort level. It also depends on the implications. In a regular relationship, meeting the family can mean going over for dinner for a few hours, and that is it – no strings attached. In a long-distance relationship, things are much different. In long-distance relationships, meeting the family means giving the family an invitation into your relationship. Because your relationship is abstract, in the sense that you cannot touch each other, your interaction and connection to the family also become abstract. The family get acquainted with you by continually being a part of your relationship and what goes on in it. Never get involved with family if you are unsure about your relationship. It is critical that you follow this rule because uncertainty tends to have a way of ruining the bond between family in a long-distance relationship. If you and your partner have relationship issues that are yet to find a resolve, be sure to resolve these issues before an introduction to the family. Be consistently on good terms with each other and with your plans for your future before introducing each other to the family.

It is a common tendency that when families of long-distance daters get involved in the relationship dynamics, suddenly everything relating to the relationship becomes family business. It happens because you and your partner live separate lives and outside of the two of you, the only other support that you both have is family. If you become each other's problem, you more than likely will not turn to each other to resolve them. Instead, you will search for your nearest and next line of support which is usually family. It is at this point that you begin to verve down a very slippery slope. Soon enough family is all over the issues in your relationship, and suddenly you realize that instead of subsiding, the problems keep getting bigger. It will get to a certain point where family now believes that they know what is best for you and try their hardest to convince you that you are better off without your partner. Your family could be right. You may be better off somewhere else, but that is beside the point. You will never know if this is true because your relationship never got the chance to reveal this to you. Family did. When this sort of thing happens with family in your relationship, try not to be too hard on your family. None of it could happen without an invitation from you to them to enter into matters of your relationship.

Deciding when to meet or invite the family into your relationship is very tricky and requires strategic planning to execute. No relationship is perfect, but your long-distance relationship must be close if you are thinking of inviting family. If you feel that family must expect some flaws, I will remind you that you are in a long-distance relationship. That is all you should need to bring you back to reality. Reality does not judge long-distance relationships; it must be perfection. Think about it; what do you work so hard every day to maintain really? The answer is perfection. It is what we all work to continue in our long-distance relationships daily, but it must never be by force. No one is perfect, and no relationship is perfect. Do not try to manufacture perfection or fake your happiness.

– Do I stay close to family? –

Again, this depends. It is never a wise idea to keep family too close to your relationship. Form a good bond with them, but do not test boundaries. Always set boundaries between your relationship with family and their involvement in your relationship, and never cross those lines. Do not, under any circumstance, discuss any aspects of your relationship with your family or with any of your partner's family members. I know it can be overly exciting when you are becoming closer to your future in-laws but you must not lose your self-control – not even a little bit. Take control of any situation that affects you. You cannot afford to let loose in this matter.

It may sound harsh, but it is for your good. As sweet and as exemplary as your relationship is with your future in-laws, they can quickly become your biggest enemy and worst nightmare. Your partner's family will always be your partner's family no matter how close you grow with them – they are still your partner's family first. Therefore, whether your relationship lasts, or does not last, your closeness to your partner's family will always be less significant.

– Family in general –

I do not mean to make family seem like the scariest thing in the world, but in a long-distance relationship, it is. In long-distance relationships, we usually expect this transition to be a lot smoother and much less complicated, especially since everyone is so far away from each other, but it is quite the opposite. It is much harder because distance causes people to want to take control of situations that do not need any additional authority. The same way you obsess about always doing everything correctly in your relationship, and always having things to say to each other, it is the same way family exaggerates and begins to obsess over your relationship. They always want to know whether it is functioning as a regular relationship would.

Maintaining a separate personal relationship with family is good for your relationship in terms of creating a diversion from topics concerning the functionality of your relationship. I am not encouraging you to keep secrets from the family, neither am I suggesting that this is the best way to handle the situation. In my experience over the last eight years, I have learned that there is high sensitivity when it comes to matters of the family in a long- distance relationship. My honest opinion to you on getting close to your partner's family is that you should only go as close for your comfort. Learn to trust your instincts – your gut feeling, because it will never lead you wrong. If you get too close, your gut will trigger a natural response that will let you know that your common-sense abilities are in a compromising situation. When you get that signal, it means that your closeness with the family has begun to cloud your better judgment and may begin to affect your relationship. At that point, you have gotten too close.

– Do I care for the family, like I do my partner? –

Only if necessary. It is typically easy to tell. It is another one of those situations where I would say you must proceed at your comfort. Set specific standards and boundaries for yourself that you will use to decide the length at which you extend your generosity from your partner to their family. It is not an immediate require- ment for you to extend anything to your partner's family, so you do not have to feel obligated to provide if you do not want to. Also, be sure that your generosity would be received well, taking into consideration that different people have different beliefs and customs that they follow.

Everything that you do in a long-distance relation- ship, whether innocently done or otherwise, can always come back and affect your relationship. As such, a crucial factor to consider is the effects that your gener- osity may have on your relationship. If you begin to provide things for your partner's family, it will create a level of expectation in the relationship, and this could potentially affect your relationship. If you decide to extend kindness to your partner's family, be prepared to be consistent. It will be the expectation once you begin on that journey. Use your discretion and gut feeling to lead you into what the right decision is to take.

FAMILY:

Worksheet

I accept whatever opinion the family has of my long-distance relationship:

Your Answer:	Ask Partner:	Total	Total
You:	Partner:	Yes:	No:
YES I NO	YES I NO		

The family is an important part of my long-distance relationship:

Your Answer:	Ask Partner:	Total	Total
You:	Partner:	Yes:	No:
YES I NO	YES I NO		

I set boundaries between my relationship with family and their involvement in my relationship:

Your Answer:	Ask Partner:	Total	Total
You:	Partner:	Yes:	No:
YES I NO	YES I NO		

I am consistent in matters concerning family:

Your Answer:	Ask Partner:	Total	Total

You:	Partner:	Yes:	No:
YES | NO	YES | NO		

I fear my relationship will not work out:

Your Answer:	Ask Partner:	Total	Total
You:	Partner:	Yes:	No:
YES | NO	YES | NO		

I worry about what family thinks of me being in a long-distance relationship:

Your Answer:	Ask Partner:	Total	Total
You:	Partner:	Yes:	No:
YES | NO	YES | NO		

I am embarrassed by my long-distance relationship:

Your Answer:	Ask Partner:	Total	Total
You:	Partner:	Yes:	No:
YES | NO	YES | NO		

My relationship seems silly to my family:

Your Answer:	Ask Partner:	Total	Total

You:	Partner:	Yes:	No:
YES | NO	YES | NO		

Answer Guide:

YES	NO
4	4

Notes:

10
– MARRIAGE PROPOSAL –

How does this work in a long-distance relationship? Does it defy all known traditions of proposing? Can a woman now propose since no one is technically going down on one knee? These questions are all great questions and important things to understand. Many couples get confused about the step of marriage in a long-distance relationship. They query themselves about how they should proceed with proposing from many miles away and if it even counts as a real proposal. The answer is yes. A long-distance proposal is as legitimate as any other proposal. When marriage comes up in a long-distance relationship, it can be a long and drawn out conversation with many beginning and end points. Once the discussion starts, there are no a permanent answers given unless someone suggests a solid plan of action.

A long-distance relationship can affect you in many ways. It can bring confusion to the people who are involved, and the stability of the relationship is what you decide to make of it. Some of the most significant concerns about approaching marriage in a long-distance relationship include having a financial safety net, fear of losing oneself, fear of complications, fear of moving too fast, and reasoning (am I doing it for the right reasons).

These are all genuine fears about marriage in long-distance relationships. If you desire to move your relationship to the next stage, then it is in your best interest to learn how to recognize these issues and work on them. You and your partner must equally share in the responsibility to fully understand the implications of a long-distance marriage before taking that step. It is a mutual effort that requires organization and determination.

– Financial safety net –

Financial safety relates to the amount of spending that will take place between you and your spouse as a married couple in a long-distance marriage. Even the deepest in pockets should consider about the robotic spending that takes place. When you are in a long-distance marriage your finances are not only separate, but they also earn separately, spend separately, and deplete separately.

If you are still wondering what I mean by this, think within yourself. Does your partner know about that new purse you bought last week? What about the new shoes and the new rims on your car? How many other things have you purchased in the past that your partner still does not know? It is critical in a long-distance relationship to always be honest and upfront about what your true desires are for your life and your relationship. To what extent are you willing to adjust your way of life and spending habits to join a union that is long distance? Are you ready to restrict yourself to plan for the future of your relationship? Do not kid yourself. A long-distance marriage can become quite an expense to pay and affording it requires a lot of compromise and self-control.

Think carefully before answering these questions if you are at the proposal stage of your relationship or if you will be approaching this stage. If you are willing, begin to plan your financial roadmap with your partner. Ensure that this plan is clear, thorough, and doable. Do not set goals for the future that is impossible to achieve. It will cause you to lose hope in your relationship and drive yourself to frustration.

It is critical in a long-distance relationship to ensure that your relationship supports your desires and vice versa. You may never be truly ready for a long-distance marriage if you do not personally prepare to play your role in the union. If you answer that you are not willing, or you are not sure, I must warn you that this type of mentality will not work in your relationship long term. I encourage you to look deep within yourself to ensure that your decisions match your priorities. Love can only do so much if you continue to neglect other aspects of your relationship. Indeed, you can be madly in love with your partner, but if you are not ready or willing to adjust to satisfy the needs of your relationship, then the relationship will not make it long term.

– Fear of losing self –

An individual is not capable of giving himself or herself to another in love if his own needs are not satisfied. The thinking behind this is simple; you cannot give out what you do not have. If I have zero dollars in my bank account and you ask me for twenty dollars, I cannot give you the twenty dollars that you ask me for because I do not have it. In the same way, if a person has not accomplished anything in life, there is nothing that they can give to their husband or wife.

I am a firm believer in this. Before you make any decisions to be married, you must ensure that you reach a point in your life where you are content. It does not mean that you must have everything all figured out because if you did, there would not be any more room for growth with your partner. It merely says that you need to have enough figured out, that it becomes an asset to your relationship, rather than a potential source of conflict.

It is critical that you practice this in a long-distance relationship. You can lose yourself to your partner or to a life that has nothing to do with the life you envisioned for yourself or that supports your needs as an individual. You feel fear when approaching marriage because you know within yourself that you have not adequately prepared for marriage. The worst thing that you can do as a human being and as a passionate lover of yourself, is to suppress your own needs. Oddly enough, this kind of self-sacrifice happens every single day. You may have done it in the past or even be doing it right now. I have certainly done this in past relationships. That is how I know that this self-sacrificing is nothing short of madness.

You cannot and will not function in a long-distance marriage if you sacrifice your own needs. You can give your partner what he or she needs without losing focus on yourself. Before bringing up the marriage talk or entertaining it from your partner, ensure that you are fulfilling your desires and working to reach the individual goals that you set for your life. Your desires are priority number one while you are still single. Marriage changes everything significantly and so even though marriage can be a beautiful and joyous adventure, it will be a disaster if you do not adequately prepare for it. The burden to perform your duty as a husband or as a wife will erase all sense of self-fulfillment if you enter marriage prematurely. It is what drives fear in couples who are in a long-distance relationship.

If you are in fear of losing yourself in marriage, it is because you are not ready to commit. You must do something about this right now while you are still single. You have the freedom to change whatever you do not like in your life in the present moment. Every decision you make right now is still about you and still only affects you. You still have the power to make your own decisions without consulting anyone first. You still have the right to be selfish, right now. Take this opportunity and run.

But you are in love? You will always be in love whether today, tomorrow, next year or forever. Love is infinite, but your life is not. You must always aim to live your best life. Remove the fear you have of getting married by working on yourself first. Once you fulfill your personal goals for your life, you will walk into marriage with unwavering confidence.

– Fear of moving too fast –

I think that as human beings we are born with a built-in trigger for self-doubt and second-guessing. We do it so very well. If you are having second guesses on approaching the marital phase in your long-distance relationship, it is ok to take the time that you need to think through this decision. Your first line of thought should be to figure out the source of your doubt. What is the question that you want to answer to be able to think through the decision you are about to make appropriately? What immediate factors of your life or your relationship cause you to get the sense that you, your partner, or both of you together are not ready to take your relationship to the next step? Is it a situation where you feel there is a need to have your options open continually? Is it your age? Do you think you are not mature enough? Are there exclusive events taking off in your life that you would like to explore before taking that step?

These are all probable sources of fear in moving towards a marriage in a long-distance relationship. Situations involving doubt creates tension and conflict in the relationship if both partners cannot agree on a course of action. The best course of action would be to provide clarity to your partner. Create a plan that confirms your commitment to your relationship and your partner, but also incorporates your desires for your life. Write out dates and timelines for when things will happen. Time is always of the essence in a long-distance relationship, and so it is urgent and crucial that you respect your partner's time by showing them that you are serious about a future with them.

***

If you feel things are moving too fast in your relationship, slow it down. If a proposal occurs and you think it is too soon, speak up. We only get a few opportunities in life to use our voice, so use it to protect yourself and your interests. Voice your concerns and expect that your partner will regard your opinion with respect.

Nothing must happen in your life that you do not want to be of existence. Love is about giving and receiving freely which also comes with the territory of saying no in some instances. Saying no should not affect your relationship in a significant way. If your partner respects your worth, they will understand and respect your desires without bringing discomfort into the relationship. The key is in the approach. If you are in the space of unquestionable love, let your partner know this. Let your partner know how much you are confident that they are the one with whom you want to spend the rest of your life. Express to them with the highest level of sensitivity that you expect that they will acknowledge and respect your feelings for the relationship to continue to function.

If your partner does not agree, it is your responsibility to find out the reason they cannot see things from your point of view. It does not mean that you should alter your feelings in any way. Your sole purpose is to listen, to understand, to acknowledge, and to state your purpose. Always keep in the back of your mind that not every problematic situation has to turn into a disagreement that leads to arguments and conflict in your relationship. Always aim to turn every ill-meaning topic or event in your relationship into a positive outcome.

– Fear of reasoning –

There are thoughts deep inside of us that has the power to encourage us and build us up or to steer us wrong and tear us down. What is even more frightening is that we control the trigger for these thoughts. You can convince yourself to do the right thing, and you can convince yourself to do the wrong thing.

The fear of reasoning refers to the source of our intentions when we think about marriage. In the context of a long-distance relationship, the reason for wanting to be married can quickly lead to misconceptions and deception. There are many instances in which getting married long-distance becomes a sole mission to gain numerous benefits such as financial gains and statuses. These instances are tremendously current and regrettably frequent. Some people make it their single mission to deceive others and to rob them of their stability and peace of mind because they believe that they have the power to do so. Be careful of intent. Always follow your gut feeling, even if it leads you in the opposite direction. Trust it.

Instances such as these are worst-case scenarios, but they are real scenarios. These unfortunate situations happen daily. Prepare yourself for these situations by keeping your eyes as open as you keep your heart. Make a conscious effort to connect and communicate with your instincts daily. Find a place of silence and relaxation – a place where you are alone with your thoughts. The first rule is never to disregard a factor based on feelings. It may seem like common sense now, but many people in long-distance relationships overlook negative elements in their relationship because they "feel" it could not be true. Do not allow yourself to fall into this trap. Break this crippling bond of giving the benefit of the doubt in situations that uncertainty should not exist in the first place. Trust your instincts to guide you onto the right path.

Be confident in your ability to conceptualize things in your life. Once you find your strengths, you will settle in a place of free flow thinking where you can see more and gain a more in-depth understanding. Do not fear marriage in your long-distance relationship. It will drain your energy. You are born with the freedom to control what happens in your life. Focus on your thoughts and your needs before you attempt to satisfy the requirements of your partner.

Aside from the possibility of ill intention, fear of reasoning can also be a result of the need for physical interaction with your partner. That means that the sole purpose of proposing marriage and subsequently marrying your partner is to close the gap of distance. That is not a good reason to get married to your long-distance partner if it is the only reason. Getting married under these pretenses will turn out to be your worst nightmare if you have not learned all that you need to know about your partner before marrying them. Do not do this. It is premature and irresponsible. Think ahead about what will happen if you finally live together with your partner under the same roof, and you come to realize that you do not like the person they are as a companion. Recovering from such a blunder would be tough. Even worse, by this point, you would have changed several things in your life or also have a brand-new outlook on life and now want different things. It is a dark and lonely place to be. Someone will lose, and someone will prevail, and there is no telling who it will be. Think critically. Take all the time you need to properly develop your rationale for getting married into a long-distance marriage. Analyze the implications to make a well-informed decision.

– Fear of complications –

Marriage is a gamble. Marriage is a gamble because even though we believe we have the perfect idea or knowledge of the person we are marrying; the facts are that people change. In any relationship, it can be difficult to manage change depending on the rate that the changes occur. In long-distance relationships, the difficulty level of managing change magnifies. In a traditional relationship where two people are living together, they can face changes head-on. They have a real chance of stopping problems that develop out of turn before it becomes a more significant problem. Unfortunately, long- distance relationships cannot afford this same convenience. Long distance relationships usually realize the changes at a much later time. This delay is severe because the changes are typically imposed on the relationship at uncontainable volumes.

You must learn to trust yourself. It is a survival skill that is useful in all aspects of life and especially in making crucial decisions such as marrying someone who lives far away. The second important thing you must do is to work on your communication skills. You must be able to communicate effectively for your relationship to grow to the next level. You must maintain this level of communication with your partner always.

Do not be afraid of complications. Arm yourself with the right tools to fight it instead. Tools including trust and good communicating skills will be the difference between a victory and a brutal loss in your relationship. Even if your relationship stays intact after a severe complication, unresolved issues may still creep up and cause more damage. Therefore, it is crucial for you to be thorough in your efforts to resolve conflict in your long-distance relationship.

A small level of indifference is good in every relationship. It can be a turning wheel in the relationship. It engages both parties to think thoroughly and critically through serious situations about the life they both want to live. These kinds of indifferences provide excellent feedback to both parties and influence them to make the best possible decisions in their relationship.

Do not try to manufacture these kinds of indifference in your relationship to create a sense of passion. Do not cultivate a significant difference between you and your partner because you believe in your mind that it can determine the strength of your bond as a couple. It is a terrible idea. These indifferences are outcomes of good situations in your relationship. It is not something that you can conjure up; it must come to your relationship from a place of mutual respect and understanding. Use it to advance the bond between you and your partner and to prove that you are ready to resolve all other indifferences that will arise in your union.

– Fear of change of heart –

The heart loves to do this thing where despite being content, it tends to wander to new avenues. Many things can change when we have too much time on our hands. It is a fact that love can move us in different directions without us having any control over it. Many of us hold on to the idea of a soulmate who is waiting somewhere in the world for us to find them. We believe that true happiness will only come once we find this person and that we must never settle for anything less.

We believe that a soulmate is someone who fits entirely into our lives now and in the future. It does not matter how you try to get around this person; they just fit you like a glove. You connect, and the bond of your relationship is near impossible to break. That is how we recognize a soulmate. The only thing is that society gives us a fairytale version that implies that this process of finding our soulmate is smooth and without much effort. That is not always true. It is entirely possible that it has just taken your current relationship a long time to mature. The problem is, you never know.

Being in a long-distance relationship is a choice. We choose to be in a long-distance relationship because we made a connection with someone who happens to live far away, and we genuinely believe deep down in the pit of our hearts that we have found our soulmate. Oddly enough, when a proposal happens, a lot of us get tummy tied and speechless. Suddenly, we begin to wonder if our partner is, in fact, the one with whom we are meant to spend over life.

The reason you feel like this is not that there is a possibility that your partner is not the one for you; although there is that possibility. You feel like this because of the ways that being in a long-distance relationship has changed you. Change is good and sometimes the only thing that saves us from ourselves. If you feel that you may reconsider, it is because you know you have not found the one who you are confident is for you. It still does not mean that your current partner is not that person. What this means is that you may have yet to find your soulmate in your current partner because your relationship has not matured to the level that unlocks this and shows you how they fit perfectly into your future. If your fear is because you know that you do not want to marry the person because he or she is not the one for you, act now while you still have a strong will to do so. Do not drag your partner along for fear of breaking their heart. If you marry them without an unobstructed vision of how they fit into your future, you will not only break their heart, but you will break your own heart as well.

– Fear of divorce –

I never understood why people always believe that refusing to take chances somehow protects their moral shields. For example, the fear of separation drives many people to stay away from ever getting married. Put a couple of thousand miles in the midst, and it becomes mission impossible to ever get them to commit to marriage. The fear of getting married and the possibility of it ending in a divorce is a fear that many people have. For some people, including myself, we believe in living our best lives which could mean separation if it is necessary.

If you fear marriage because you worry about getting divorced, the first step in getting rid of this fear is to accept divorce for what it is. If you are asking yourself why you should accept the thing that you are most afraid of, the answer is simple. The only way to get rid of fear is to face it. I promise you. There is no other way. Any alternate course of action will include living with fear for the rest of your life. If you have come this far into this book, that simply means that you and I have developed a level of trust – you trust me to help you maintain and grow a healthy long-distance relationship. Therefore, if you trust me, trust me when I tell you that you must accept divorce for what it is to relieve yourself from the fear of it.

Accepting divorce for what it is, does not mean that you believe in it. You merely recognize that it exists. To receive the idea of divorce, you must first acknowledge that there are genuine reasons for why people get divorced. Again, you do not have to believe in this; you must recognize that there are justifiable reasons why people get divorced. After you acknowledge this, think of all the reasons why people get divorced. Think of the reasons that are good, bad, trivial, and the ones that do not make any sense.

When you think of the reasons, analyze them based solely on common sense. Think about the type of people who are engaged in these types of divorces. Think about their personalities, their likes and dislikes, their hopes, and dreams, and most importantly, think about their fears. While you are actively participating in this thinking exercise, do not compare these people to yourself. Do not think about any aspect of your life while you are examining theirs. It is especially important that you keep your opinions of them separate from the views of yourself and of your relationship. If you include yourself in your thinking about their circumstances, this process will become confusing to you.

Once you have completed the exercise and are not actively analyzing anyone else, begin to examine yourself using the information you gathered about the types of people who get divorced. What are your personalities, likes and dislikes, hopes, and dreams and fears? Now and only now, you may begin the comparison between other people and yourself. How do you measure up to people who get divorced? Are the foundations of your bond with your partner significant enough to support your hopes, dreams, and fears of being in a marital union? Do you possess the qualities to grow a martial union actively? What are your capabilities? What are the unique abilities of your relationship?

The core of relieving the fair of divorce is to believe in yourself. Marriage has two people in and so it always has double the chance of survival. Do not sell yourself short or undermine your capabilities as a leading factor in your relationship. Marriage primarily centers on mutual support. You must be determined to remain in your marriage to stay married. Instead of fearing divorce, rely on your strengths to assure that your marriage will last.

On women making the first move. Women can always propose no matter what geographical distance exist between her and her partner. Being in a long-distance relationship is not an escape for women to propose marriage to a man. A woman can always propose to a man if she feels within her heart that they are for each other. The same thing goes for men. Only make the step to propose if you genuinely believe that your partner is the one for you.

– Considering marriage –

Remain focused on all the other crucial factors that must be well-thought-out when considering a long-distance marriage. It is not easy to maintain a long-distance marriage. It is challenging, and it comes with much emotional confusion. Planning a life together over a long distance comes with many territories. Many things need to be in place before making that step forward. There must be a plan of execution for the transition from living separately to living under the same roof. This change will be intimidating, and you must prepare for it.

The good news is you can start preparing right now. Begin to plan the life that you see for you and your partner and continuously share this knowledge with them to get their input. Get your partner actively involved in this planning by contributing to the plan. By doing this, you ensure that the life you plan is a life that is ideal for both you and to your partner. It also serves as practice collaborating as a unit. Starting this transition in your thinking from these preliminary stages will be beneficial to your union.

You must begin to train your mind to think as a part of a marital union. Get into the thinking and habit of making decisions based on consideration for another human being. Realize that marriage means that you are responsible for all the outcomes in the life of another person. In the business of marriage what you do is no longer about you. Your actions must now consider your spouse. That is why it is essential to ensure that you have met your personal goals before considering marriage. In a long-distance marriage, you will need to function as if it were a traditional marriage and do so from a distance.

***

A marriage proposal is an incredibly special event whether done long distance or otherwise. When done from a distance it has the same meaning and is of the equal importance as any other time. Your most significant responsibility is to ensure that there is no room for confusion from either you or your partner. If you are planning to propose while apart, ensure that you and your partner are both on the same page; this event should not be a total surprise to them. When you are ready, propose. Your proposal should be as special and as spontaneous as any other. Bring spontaneity to your partner anywhere in the world they may be. Get creative and think outside of the box; you may be far away, but the delivery flower shop is right around the corner from your partner. You may be far away, but the support of close friends and family of your beloved is closer to them and can assist you. Plan as though you are present. Make your beloved feel as if you are there. Exercise creativity. You can do it.

If you and your partner are secure in your union and have an active communication structure within your relationship, your future is sure to be a bright future. The key is to nurture this bond continually. Start doing this from right now. If you neglect certain aspects of your relationship, now is the perfect opportunity to make it right. If you continuously do things to cause the topic of marriage to be harder than it must be, talk to your partner right now to make it right.

If there is absolutely no doubt in your mind that you are genuinely in love and that the strength of your love can withstand all obstacles, you have a solid foundation to build a lifelong marriage. Faith can move mountains. If you have enough confidence and strong will, you can achieve anything in your life. Go at a steady pace. Be confident in your ability to know what is right for you.

MARRIAGE PROPOSAL:

Worksheet

I am willing to adjust my way of life to be in a long-distance marriage:

Your Answer:	Ask Partner:	Total	Total
You:	Partner:	Yes:	No:
YES | NO	YES | NO		

My relationship supports my desires:

Your Answer:	Ask Partner:	Total	Total
You:	Partner:	Yes:	No:
YES | NO	YES | NO		

My desires support my relationship:

Your Answer:	Ask Partner:	Total	Total
You:	Partner:	Yes:	No:
YES | NO	YES | NO		

My decisions match my priorities:

Your Answer:	Ask Partner:	Total	Total
You:	Partner:	Yes:	No:
YES | NO	YES | NO		

I connect to my instincts daily:

Your Answer:	Ask Partner:	Total	Total
You:	Partner:	Yes:	No:
YES | NO	YES | NO		

I am suspicious of my partner's intent for being in the relationship:

Your Answer:	Ask Partner:	Total	Total
You:	Partner:	Yes:	No:
YES | NO	YES | NO		

I mostly provide financial support for my relationship:

Your Answer:	Ask Partner:	Total	Total
You:	Partner:	Yes:	No:
YES | NO	YES | NO		

I sometimes neglect certain aspects of my relationship:

Your Answer:	Ask Partner:	Total	Total
You:	Partner:	Yes:	No:

YES	NO	YES	NO		

Answer Guide:

YES	NO
5	3

Notes:

11
– SEX –

In these modern times, many things have changed in long-distance relationships. One of these things is the way in which we look at sex in a long-distance relationship. Long-distance couples are expecting more effort from each other in keeping the relationship running as healthy as possible including the constant satisfaction of sexual desires. In long-distance relationships, couples can now have their need for sexual gratification met regardless of the distance.

The expectation to fulfill sexual desires even from a distance comes from the desperate need to convince ourselves that we want to remain in a long-distance relationship. We are all adults, and we need sex. It is the number one thing that scares us away from long-distance relationships and the number one thing that causes us to end our long-distance relationships. To ensure that this does not happen, a lot of long-distance couples aim for perfection and end up wearing themselves out and becoming annoyed with the lifestyle and bored with themselves. It is at this point that reinforcements need to be in order.

Women have primarily had the better options in sex substitution but welcome to 2018, a year of fake vaginas and manufactured life-size sex dolls. These modern upgrades have certainly changed the game for men in long-distance relationships. In the meantime, the fake penises are getting bigger with each shipment, and the vibrating bullets keep rolling off the shelves. We are in a new world of sex where we can choose whether we want pleasure from our partner or by ourselves. All these new machines and toys have allowed us to be so efficient that we do not even have a practical use for our partners anymore. I remain incredibly excited over all these new and exciting developments, and I support whichever method you perceive fit to practice in your relationship. The most important thing with regards to sex substitution in your long-distance relationship is to practice fairness.

When you begin to think about the ways you can substitute sex in your long-distance relationship use your partner as inspiration. You aim to please them and so considering them when making your plans will allow you to tailor those plans specific to their needs. Also, consider the reciprocity of your kindness. In other words, ensure that you are receiving the same or better from your partner that you give to them. There must be mutual excitement, mutual effort, joint participation, and a shared desire to satisfy each other sexually from a distance.

In a long-distance relationship, sex becomes a state of mind. It is an adjustment that you must learn to cope with by reducing the distraction that comes from the need for it. Unbelievably, many people in long-distance relationships do learn how to satisfy themselves with the absence of sex in their relationships. Many people in long-distance relationships cope on a day to day basis; going weeks, months and even years without a touch. It may seem unusual, but it does happen every day in the modern world of long-distance relationships. There are many ways and methods that you can use to substitute for sex in your relationship and be satisfied.

– Other considerations –

Another consideration is that you may not be as open to experimenting sexually with your partner, especially if you have not met them face to face yet. My recommendation to you is never to stretch yourself too thin. If you have not reached the comfort level in your relationship where you can consider the idea of opening to your partner sexually, do not force yourself to be that person. The same goes even if you have reached that comfort level but choose not to participate. The choice is entirely up to you to make. It is an innovative idea to have a healthy amount of sexual arousal in your relationship on a constant basis; however, you should never force yourself to participate if you do not feel comfortable.

– Practice fairness –

The one thing you cannot afford to be in your relationship is selfish. You must always have your limits and set ambitious standards in your relationship, but also consider your partner as much as possible and as fair as possible for your comfort. Be willing to try something at least once in your life. Indulge your partner now and then in the unique things that make them go wild. Be passionate about satisfying your partner's sexual drive. It is a fantastic experience if you commit to giving it your best.

Set rules and let your partner know what your limits are. Let your partner know what happens if they violate those limits. Start small and increase as your comfort level expands. As you build trust in your partner, this process will become much more comfortable. Keep the subject of sex as light as possible, as often as possible. Build a relationship where the subject of sex can be a part of your conversations without any awkwardness. The more you can accentuate your speech with a hint of sexual implication, the more you can keep the mind and body of your partner aroused.

Take Matters into Your Own Hands. If all else fails, you can always take matters into your own hands – literally. The need for affection and sex can become crippling in a long-distance relationship. Sometimes even after you try all the methods and ways of reinventing sexual arousal with your partner and have success, the desire for sex makes a complete turn and has you wanting for more. Suddenly you are in a 360 degrees cycle of trying to satisfy your need for sex.

This never-ending need for sex can undoubtedly become stressful on your relationship. Sometimes the need occurs back to back, day to day and even hour to hour. It all depends on what your appetite for sex is. Funny enough, our desire for sex grows to ridiculous volumes when we are in a long-distance relationship. It is frightening really. Rest assured that there are many things that you and your partner can do together that helps to soothe the craving. Do not distract yourself with suspicions about whether your partner may get the urge to fulfill their sexual needs elsewhere. Do not preoccupy your mind with this. Sexual gratification happens because of your partner. If you have sexual desires for someone else or if your partner has sexual desires for someone else, the problem is not your relationship; the problem is both of you and what you both genuinely desire personally.

In all my years of dating long-distance, I have never cheated on any of my partners or even had the desire to do so. I did not lust off every man that I saw on the street, neither did I have any willingness to pay attention to the ones that came looking. It was not hard for me to do. I knew what I wanted and what I wanted was my partner. So instead of letting my mind idle to other places, I channeled my sexual frustrations into creating sexual pleasure for myself and my partner, using a lot of interactive methods that involved my partner.

– Tasking –

Oh yes, tasks! Normal couples do foreplay. They create alter-egos, dress up as sexy villains and do naughty things to each other in unusual places. You can do the same thing in your relationship without distance ever getting in the way. The reality remains that you and your partner cannot touch each other physically, but if you commit yourselves to try something new and put your mind to it, you will hardly even miss the real touch. Get creative. You can still dress up in your costume as if you were putting it on for your partner. Bring your character to life by creating an entire experience for your partner.

Assign tasks to each other. You can do this every day, every other day or even once a week; whatever suits your sexual appetite. Give a command – a sexual command. The idea is that your partner will control every aspect of your sexual experience in that specific moment. You must listen and give control of yourself entirely to your partner. Take turns and be sure to isolate turns. The tasks that you assign can be anything, at any time, and at any intensity. The tasks you choose to assign to your partner is ultimately your choice. You aim to please, and so you must ensure that your instructions result in pleasure for your partner.

If you decide to attempt this, always remember that honesty and openness are the biggest players in this game. You must be open and honest with each other throughout the entire process. If something does not please you or if a set of instructions did not do anything for you, talk your partner through doing it at the right level of intensity that you desire. This exercise is as much about building on your communication skills with each other, as it is about achieving pleasure. You improve your communication skills by learning to rely on each other for support and guidance throughout the experience.

– Role play phone sex –

If tasking is not your thing or it is just not working out as well for you as you would hope, you still have the option of going back to the basics of phone sex. Phone sex is an oldie but still reaps the same benefits. Even regular couples who live down the street from each other have phone sex. In fact, couples who live together indulge in it sometimes as well. Unlike tasking, phone sex is a more interactive form of sexual imitation. You do not have to go out of your way to buy any sex toys or costumes if that is not your thing.

Another beautiful thing about phone sex is that it usually puts noticeably less pressure on partners when they fully participate in it. The mutual instructiveness of the entire process allows you to be in a relaxed and open state as you lead each other into creating sexual satisfaction for yourselves. Your partner's focused, and soft-spoken tone will cause your body to release tension which allows you to become more interactive with them. That is how good phone sex always starts.

If you have a timid personality and cannot bring yourself around to "talk dirty," you are going to find that it will be difficult to connect with your partner sexually. If you do not know how to "talk dirty," or do not have enough experience and it makes you feel silly, there are ways that you can practice how to become better. If you usually become speechless when your partner tells you to talk dirty, practice a few warm-ups beforehand by sending stimulating messages to your partner first. Doing this allows you more time to put your thoughts together. There is no time pressure to think quickly since your partner is not on the phone waiting for your response. Use the text messages as practice on how to become descriptive with your words. Use your partner as inspiration.

If you have not met your partner in person just yet,

use what you know about your partner from pictures and videos that they may have sent you. Use your imagination to visualize "dirty" and romantic things that your partner could do to you or that you could do to them. For example, think about how their lips move when they talk. Imagine what those lips are like when your partner is kissing you. Imagine their touch. How does it feel? Think about how the touch of their hands feels on your skin. Imagine how the saliva from their tongue penetrates your skin when they kiss you on your neck.

If you have been with your partner and especially if you have had sex with them, this should be much easier for you to bring to reality. In your case, you only need half the imagination it takes to envision these images because you already know what you and your partner are capable of sexually. What you must utilize is your memory. Use your memory to trace everything that your partner has done to you during sex. Once you have that image in your mind amplify it. If your partner usually performs oral sex on you, intensify that in your text. Instead of what they typically do, request something ten times more complex that will increase the pleasure. The more outrageous you are with your sexual requests, the more you will capture the attention of your partner. Make it fun and competitive. For example, if you tell your partner what you want, and they tell you that you are crazy, pull their strings by implying that they are acting cowardly, so they will be determined to prove you wrong.

Once you build confidence through text messaging, begin to say it aloud. Start by dropping a sensual line or phrase in the middle of a perfectly polite conversation. When you are having conversations in bed at night, begin to use the speech that you sent in your texts to stimulate your partner as they are going to bed. Tell your partner about all the things that you imagine them doing to you, and you do to them. Remind them of all the things they have done to you and that you have done to them. Tell them what you like or imagine that you would want and why you want them. Compliment your partner on things that they do very well or believe that they would do well. Find out where they learned it from or if they can do it in real life, and engage them by asking them to teach you. The point of all of this is to remain engaged with your partner and to learn more about each other through these mentally stimulating exercises.

If you have not met your partner, transitioning from regular talk to talking about sex and having phone sex is an absolute daunting experience. Some people can breeze through this process smoothly, but even I have reservations sometimes. If you are with someone that their temperament can be all over the place, it is hard to know when or if they are in a frame of mind to talk about or participate in any sexually arousing activities.

You may also fear what they will think of you for bringing up sex. If both people in the relationship are holding back and just going with the flow, the conversations in the relationship will continue to draw out until you both lose interest. Suddenly you conclude that your partner is not into sex, or not into you because they are not bringing up the subject first. It is one of the many brutal and silly games that we often play in long-distance relationships. It is unnecessary and a waste of precious time.

***

The whole point in having phone sex is to use your imagination to connect with your partner. It is also a way for you to achieve satisfaction in your relationship, regardless of the distance that is between you and your partner. You can choose to appreciate the idea of phone sex as an alternative way to connect with your partner. In a long-distance relationship, you are not within geographical reach of your partner to be able to touch them physically. You will realize that you must depend on the creativity of your mind to feel your partner spiritually. To do this, you must continuously train your imaginative mind.

– Good ole sexting –

Sexting is an alternative to having phone sex if you really cannot do the live "dirty" talk. Sexting is the same

183

as phone sex, except it is by text. If you are in a long-distance relationship, sexting is automatically apart of your vocabulary. Either you initiate it, or your partner will ask you for it. Sexting comes in different forms. It can be anything from an explicit text message to sending nude images.

I enjoy an interactive episode of intense sexting, but my generosity stops at sending nudes. Whether it is to your boyfriend or girlfriend or husband or wife; always remain conscious of the individuals who have access to such sensitive information about you. There is a lot of the danger that comes with sending such images of yourself across an electronic medium. Consider the trustworthiness of the recipient. Can you trust your partner with this information? If you broke up tomorrow, is your partner the kind of person who would make those images public? Whether by intention or by mistake, the risk of exposure is significantly high.

If you have not met your partner face to face, you must allow your better judgment to make the call on whether you can live with your conscience knowing that such damaging information about you is somewhere out in the world. There is also a chance that such images may end up putting you in compromising situations even if it is not the intention. Accidents do happen, and they can occur even while the images are in your possession. The rate at which things accidentally end up on social media is alarming. You can never be too sure. If you decide to send these images to your partner, take the necessary precautions to protect your interest. Start at a good pace and build up.

You have a Choice. In my eight years of dating long-distance, I have never sent a nude picture of myself to anyone of partners although they asked. The difference is I made it clear early in the relationship that I would never send a naked or half-naked picture of myself to anyone. I have done everything else under the sun including sexy lingerie pictures, side boobs, and ample cleavage. These all serve as props in my relationship. They complement my words in helping to stimulate my partner sexually. Besides, it is never any fun giving your partner exactly what they ask for in a sexual scenario.

Being in a long-distance relationship can sometimes cloud our better judgment. We consume ourselves with trying to make our relationship work, and sometimes we are willing to do so at all cost. Always have a mind of your own. Know what is wrong from what is right and when enough is enough. Take control of situations that have a direct effect on you.

– Erotica –

Erotic artistry is any artistic work that creates sexual stimulation. It includes things such as paintings, film, music, and writing. Erotica is when you listen to the

Boys II Men single, "I'll Make Love to You" and send it to your partner with the intention of letting them know what you will do to them and how you will do it the next time you see them. It is also the lovemaking scenes in films that you send to partner when you want to send them a message without saying a word. In writing, it is using your imagination to tell your partner about the incredibly detailed ways in which you will both make love to each other.

Think of erotic artistry as art that expresses an art. Use it to communicate the art of lovemaking in its physical absence. Erotica is about using all the resources in your environment to connect with your partner on a deep and intimate level. Having the ability to summon the things of nature is an enrichening life ability. Being able to take anything from nature and use it to stimulate your partner sexually is a talent that is rare. Once you have that power, there is nothing that you cannot do to please your partner.

– Use heightened senses –

Activating your senses is another way to connect sexually with your long-distance partner. Heightened senses mean that you put your memory to work in bringing pieces of your past experiences into the present moment. In a long-distance relationship, this is an ability mastered with practice. Once you learn this, you can bring any recent event into your reality as if it is happening at the moment.

I have trained my mind to a point where I can bring a moment from years ago into my reality, and it will seem real. It is my favorite tool for releasing sexual tensions at nights when I find I cannot go to sleep. I think of my partner at a specific time and everything that he is doing at that moment. I focus on it and bring it into the present. If I am sad in the past; I am sad in the present. If I feel pleasure in the past; I feel pleasure in the present. Before you try to concentrate on your partner, you must block out everything that is around you; good or bad. To become increasingly sexually aroused by the thoughts of your partner your focus must be solely on them. If you have been in the arms of your partner before, try to remember exactly how they smell. Use your memory to bring you back to that place and bring that smell into the present. Repeat this for things like their touch, voice, hold, kiss, and of course sex.

– *Fantasies* –

Everyone is different. No one remedy will work for all people, but there are universal qualities we can learn to use to manage in these inopportune moments. It will require activating your senses. I am a sensual woman. I use my memory combined with my thoughts to create fantasies. I can make my last encounter with my partner feel as though I am in the moment again. It is the power of memory and the power of the human mind. When my partner and I were apart for months at a time and one point, one entire year; this technique was faithful in its usefulness. To get through these tough times, you must fully expound your memory. Try to remember as many details as you can. What you are trying to do is to recreate sex between you and your partner. Recreate the same atmosphere that you would be in if you were with your partner to set the tone of the environment. Is it usually quiet, or noisy? Do you usually have sex on the floor or bed or couch? Once you create this domain, turn off the senses that you do not need, and that could potentially distract you.

The number one thing that comes to mind would be to close your eyes. Your vision continually puts your brain to work and, in this situation, your memory needs the full attention of your brain to pull the details that it needs to bring your experience to the present moment.

Close your eyes and relax into the experience. When you are resting, think of a time with your partner that made you feel happy. Zone in on this. Let your mind take you to that place. What does it look like in this place? What is the smell? Taste? What is your partner doing? Is your partner touching you? If so, follow the touch. Open your eyes and look at the touch. It will help you to bring the touch into your present. Listen to the words that are spoken and dissolve them into feeling.

Use your sense of touch, smell, taste, and hearing in your real world to magnify the fantasy that you have created. If you need the faculty of sight, in case your imagination wants you to move around, open your eyes.

The creation of fantasies is an authentic and immensely powerful coping tool in long-distance relationships. Do not underestimate the power of it. You may say that it is different from the real thing, and you are right, but it does feel close. Like everything else in a long-distance relationship, coping methods are a means to an end. It is a safety net to get you to the next time you see your partner face to face.

The creation of fantasies can do a lot for your mental state with or without your partner. The fantasies that you create when you are a part will always remain in your memory. You are not only creating these fantasies to get you through the night; you are creating them for future sexual benefits in your relationship. The authority and influence from these fantasies reactivate once you are with your partner.

If you are in a relationship where you only see your partner for a few days with months in between, you will appreciate the power of fantasy. Likewise, if you are a couple that only has hours to see each other with months in between, you are entirely aware of the importance of creating memories to be able to replay them in your mind when you are apart. Once you learn how

to create fantasies to cope, use these fantasies to enhance your physical attraction to your partner. This
way, the next time you see them, they will have something to remember you.

Let your creative Juices Run. Get your creative juices
running by thinking about ways to spice up your long-
distance relationship sex life. It all comes down to your
willingness and the amount of effort that you put into
it. There are many things that you can create between
you and your partner that will always keep you both on
your feet and curious about what will come next in your
relationship. Now and then, get out a pen and a piece of
paper and jot down ideas of things that you and your
partner can do together to keep your daily interaction
constant. Make this list of things with a level of compet-
itiveness that provides incentives for you and your
partner to want to do them and want to stick with the
process.

Talk about sex ALL the time. I am not sure of how a lousy
stigma got attached to the sex talk between adults but
talking about sex has become a severe point of contention in adult relationships. Especially in a long-distance
relationship, it is hard to know when the appropriate
time is to discuss sex, from when the time is inconvenient. To curve this uncertainty, you must build an open
relationship that you can state your desires at any point

in time without feeling silly for doing so.

Drop Hints. Once you get past the phase of building a safe environment to discuss sex in your relationship; find diverse ways of introducing the idea of sex to your partner. It does not have to be the hot and heavy dialogue that you usually use, and I do not recommend it for an everyday talk. Change your dialogue to something that is light on the ear and easy to move through. These hints are to be precisely that – hints. They should not prolong; neither should they turn into a conversation. If your partner tries to make a conversation out of something that you said about sex, answer vaguely and do not linger on the question. When you do this on occasion, it keeps a constant flow of sexual stimulation in your relationship daily. It is just the right amount to hold you over until you see each other again.

The hints should peak your partner's interest – nothing more. The thought will continue to linger with your partner for the rest of the day, night, and the days to come. Even after a few days, your partner will still want to find out. When they ask for the second time, remember that you are in control of the situation. Set your rules. Give your conditions for when, and under what circumstances you will elaborate on the subject. Pique their interest.

SEX

Worksheet

I exercise my imaginative mind in my relationship:

Your Answer:	Ask Partner:	Total	Total
You:	Partner:	Yes:	No:
YES | NO	YES | NO		

I think of creative ways to connect with my partner daily:

Your Answer:	Ask Partner:	Total	Total
You:	Partner:	Yes:	No:
YES | NO	YES | NO		

I interact with my partner sexually:

Your Answer:	Ask Partner:	Total	Total
You:	Partner:	Yes:	No:
YES | NO	YES | NO		

I feel safe to talk about sex with my partner:

Your Answer:	Ask Partner:	Total	Total
You:	Partner:	Yes:	No:
YES | NO	YES | NO		

My partner relieves my sexual tensions:

Your Answer:	Ask Partner:	Total	Total
You:	Partner:	Yes:	No:
YES | NO	YES | NO		

I worry about my partner cheating due to the need for sex:

Your Answer:	Ask Partner:	Total	Total
You:	Partner:	Yes:	No:
YES | NO	YES | NO		

I am never sure if I can approach my partner to talk about sex:

Your Answer:	Ask Partner:	Total	Total
You:	Partner:	Yes:	No:
YES | NO	YES | NO		

I fear what my partner thinks of me if I always bring up the topic of sex first:

Your Answer:	Ask Partner:	Total	Total

You:	Partner:	Yes:	No:
YES | NO	YES | NO		

Answer Guide:

YES	NO
5	3

Notes:

12
– MARRIED COUPLES –

I know exactly how you feel at this moment. I have been there, and I have done it. Do not waste too much time trying to consider how you ended up in a long-distance marriage because you will get a headache.

– Second guesses/Insecurity –

Your marriage is real; you know this more than anyone else. Do not allow self-doubt, family doubts, friends, or even society make you feel differently. Do not assume that because your marriage is long-distance, it is immune to marital issues. This journey is anything but smooth sailing. In fact, you have slightly more issues than an average traditional marital union. These issues come from various aspects of your relationship, the prime element being the communicative skills that you adopt in your relationship. Lack of effective communication in a long-distance marriage is like falling over a never-ending edge. You will get to the peak of frustration and watch yourself fall off the edge and never land anywhere. It is unsatisfying and excruciatingly painful.

Another source of contention in long-distance marriages are insecurities. Insecurity is a ruthless disease. It creeps up on you in the most unexpected ways and at the most inconvenient times. Insecurity usually comes from lack of trust or broken trust, but in long-distance relationships, insecurity can come from anywhere at any time. Insecurity masks itself and can transfer itself to any aspect of your relationship. It is what causes you to have constant and progressive trust issues in your long-distance marriage. It makes you believe that there is a negative component in your long-distance relationship, whether it exists.

Many marriages do have husbands and wives that do not respect, listen to, or care about each other and this fuels insecurity in these marriages. The key is to rigorously evaluate the dynamics of your relationship to ensure that your marriage constantly has the necessary qualities that it will require to grow into the future.

If you must ask yourself if your partner respects you, you already know that they do not. Analyze your marriage to ensure that the component of respect had already been established and maintained over the course of the entire relationship. It is quite easy to miss these signs earlier on in a relationship and many people end up marrying into broken and dysfunctional marriages because of this. Some people are even of the perception that marriage will instantly solve these already existing issues, and this thinking is incorrect. Marriage cannot resolve your personal or relationship problems. It is never a wise idea to enter marriage for this reason.

Do not underestimate your instinct. Signing a legally binding document does not stop ill-intentioned people from entering or altering your life. The healthiest way to move forward in your long-distance marriage is to maintain trust. Establish an open atmosphere in your relationship where you can express your feelings and engage in productive conversations that will benefit you, your spouse, and the longevity of your union. Repeat this step for every other question that you ask yourself about your spouse.

– Look to the future –

Talk about the future with your partner frequently and remain excited about all the plans that you both made for your future. Be passionate about even the simplest things such as your scheduled skype video chat or the next time you will see each other. The nurturing of excitement in your long-distance marriage can inspire hope for the future of your relationship. Keep your mind and heart active and busy, by distracting it with time-consuming things that are of value to you, your spouse, and your union.

Encourage continuous laughter between you and

your spouse. The memories will linger in your mind constantly and serve as a reminder to you both of why you commit yourself to each other. It will create inspiration for you daily and allow you to smile when the burdens of a long-distance marriage befall on you in certain moments.

When you linger in bed before falling asleep, use those few minutes to dream up the perfect life for you and your spouse. Keep these thoughts in your consciousness and work diligently to make them real. Meditate on your love story. Remember the moment you met your spouse, the things you shared, the hopes and dreams that you shared, and the ideas that led you both to the altar. Recall the promises that cemented your foundation. These include plans for children, buying a home, or starting a business; whatever plans and promises that you both made to each other as an agreement to endure this process. Connect these reasonings with your goals to get inspiration to remain committed to your marriage until you reach your end goal.

One of my favorite things to plan is trips. It is my preferred method of focusing on the future. I always plan one trip after the other, and each trip centers around my partner. Preparing from one trip to the next ignites excitement in your relationship. This excitement influences anticipation in your relationship that stays with you until the moment you see each other. Anticipation inspires spontaneity which assures that you will have the most special time of your life once you are in the arms of your partner. As soon as you arrive at your spouse, or your spouse comes to you, start outlining the next trip together. The idea behind keeping busy with planning for future trips is so that you and your spouse can maintain a sense of accomplishment as a married couple. It will give both of you a sense of teamwork and increase your level of communication.

– Close the gap –

Being apart must not and cannot be a prolonged phase in your marriage. You cannot have a long-distance marriage for the rest of your lives. By the time you approach marriage in your long-distance relationship, a clear plan must be in place for you and your partner to be together in the same physical space within one to two years.

Closing the gap will depend on your circumstance. In my case, I lived in the United States while my spouse lived in another country. My plan then was to get my spouse with me here in the United States, as that option made a lot more sense. I could not join my spouse in his country because there were no financial gains there and so there would not have been a good future for us to live there. That was the deciding factor in my marriage. Much of the guesswork was not necessary because it was an obvious best choice.

For many other couples, however, you may have different options available to you. It could quite possibly be that it would be better if you went to your spouse's country or if you both choose a separate country altogether. The most important thing to consider is that you and your partner must decide on this first before you begin to formulate a plan of action. Decide what is more conducive to the long-term survival of your marriage and to reaching your end goal.

Have a plan. In a long-distance marriage, you must have a solid plan. As you grow in your marriage and experience a variety of changes, this plan will start to evolve and become a bigger and more elaborate version of your original plan. The number one expectation in your marriage is that you and your partner will plan for your financial future.

Long distance relationships need mobility. It is even more critical once the relationship transitions into marriage. Marital unions attract high expenses, and a long-distance marriage is no different. Your marriage will require financial stability to function well. You need an appropriate budget, and personal limits, to adequately maintain a long-distance marriage. That is what will secure a long-term future for your relationship. Love is the most important aspect of a relationship; on this point, I firmly agree. However, love cannot save a long-distance marriage that does not have a solid plan for growing into the future.

In a long-distance marriage, finances become the most critical factor in every aspect of the relationship – considering the cost of plane fares, hotel stays, and entertainment that falls between the time of transition. These are all expenses that you must account for in addition to making preparations for your permanent physical transition to be together. Start the planning for this transition now. Begin to put things into motion. Approach your spouse immediately and begin to plan financially for the transition to being under the same roof.

Get a feel for living with your spouse. One of the biggest mistakes that long-distance couples make is to marry someone and find out later that they cannot cope with or live with their spouse. You can avoid this situation if you are willing to invest your time into finding out as much as you need to about your partner before marriage.

Use your vacation time to be with each other in one physical space. Skip the all-inclusive hotels and opt to stay at home or if in a foreign country, get an apartment that has the full amenities as would a house. Use this time to learn about your partner's mannerisms. Observe their temperament. Find out what they like in a home and what they do not like. Create an atmosphere that imitates a marital home to practice how you and your partner will coexist under one roof.

Once you and your spouse create your domain, expect a shift in personality, habits, morals, and behaviors. It is a natural occurrence that accompanies the new responsibilities that come with owning and operating a domain. Use this opportunity to resolve any unexpected issues that arise from living together under the same room. Each time you travel to your partner or your partner goes to you, use this time to fix smaller issues that come up in the relationship. Doing this will prepare you for the more significant battles that you will face in your relationship in the future.

When you experiment this way together, many tension- brewing topics will come up in the relationship. Things such as leaving the toilet seat up, to more complex issues such as who is spending too much. When these tensions come up, your first line of action should be to take responsibility for the role that you played. In a situation involving spending, this is also the best opportunity to have a thorough conversation with your spouse about finances.

Make no mistake; cold feet did not bid you goodbye at the altar. You will continue to experience this as you settle into your marriage. Cold feet will attack your personal space and send you into shock. It will proceed to activate your pride and turn your self-righteousness into self-destruction. It is a regular occurrence in any new adventure. You should not be afraid of it, but you must not allow it to influence your relationship dynamics either. There is an incredible opportunity that lies beneath every disagreement in your relationship. The opportunity is that one unique chance that you get to turn every unpleasant situation into the right circumstance and grow stronger together as a couple.

– Prepare for the transition –

When you find yourself in a disagreement with your spouse, pause. Take three deep breaths and then say, "I love you." These three words will trigger a calmness in both you and your spouse. The tension will subside slowly as you both reduce your tempers. Always avoid blunt confrontation with your spouse at all cost. It will only sever the line of communication between you and hinder you from effectively getting your point across to your spouse in a positive way.

Build a stable bond with your partner to prepare for the transition in your relationship. Talk about things that are uncomfortable and strange. Build an emotional bond to replace the physical bond that is missing and commit to it. Always keep in mind that your marriage is as real as any and so it will be tested as any. It is just worst off for you because you continuously have a distance to contend with, but do not let this discourage you. You must be committed to making your marriage work. It must be something that you want to accomplish, not for your spouse or any other outside factors, for yourself.

Start today by making your plan. Start with a system of financial execution. Plan small futuristic events such as the next time you will fly to see your spouse or vice versa. Plan your next "bae-cation," or the next birthday surprise, to keep your mind actively focused on your spouse and your relationship. Start putting the plans into motion for the blueprint of the rest of your lives together. Answer questions together such as where you both will be in two years, where you will live, and how you will live. Plan for a secure future in which you will both live comfortably.

– Making the transition –

You must take into consideration, all the aspects of this physical transition and how it will affect your relationship. The first step is to decide where you will live as a couple. Once you figure this out, you can begin to make strategic plans based on this decision. Once you select a country or a specific city, start to research on all the information that you will need to make the transition.

Study things such as the unique laws of the country that you will live in as a union. More than likely, there will be a need to complete an immigration process. Begin to research on how this process will work based on the country you live in currently. Research things such as the cost of completing such procedures, and the timeframe that it will take to do so. Take this into consideration when accounting for the level of financial support that this process will require the relationship. Usually, in the process of immigration, the partner who must complete the process will not be able to work and provide equal support to the household. Take this into consideration when planning and making a budget for this transition.

Take this process seriously. Your relationship will encounter a series of difficulties indefinitely if you enter this transitional period prematurely. Also take into consideration, the unique stresses that this process will place on your bond and on your relationship. Do not be naïve. Your marriage will become stressful. It is not a question. It is a fact. There will be stress on the partner who will have to temporarily sit at home, unable to earn income; and the partner who is working, will become stressed because they must juggle working to support the family while still keeping up with their role in the marriage.

Be prepared to face these unique challenges in this transition. Practice patience with each other. You will need this when making the change. When you are living under the same roof, you will learn a lot of new and exciting things about your partner. Some you will love and some you will despise. It is essential that you approach the unpleasant aspects of your union in a structured pattern. Do not address it immediately. Take a few minutes or even a day to think things over to see if you still feel the same way. Many times when we react to situations, our feelings usually changes afterward. We begin to look at the situation in a separate way, and we start to change our thinking towards it.

Be kind to each other after the transition. Full your home with laughter and good vibes. Go out and explore your environment. Have new experiences together and genuinely enjoy each other's company.

Marriage is not a marathon. Do not feel rushed to do more than what is necessary to keep your relationship running smoothly. Do not over think it. Consistently believe in the abstract of love. Do not be distracted by things on the outside of your marriage. It will only divert you from your purpose. Your long-distance marriage is just as real and just as important as any other marriage. Always love, care for, and respect your spouse, regardless of the distance that exists between you.

13
– PRECAUTIONS –

It is always a wise idea to take maximum precautions in any relationship that you enter. This principle becomes even more critical when you are dating long-distance. You must be careful at all time. There are many benefits to maintaining a long-distance relationship if you are receiving what you need from the relationship. Do not make excuses in your relationship if you are not getting the things that you desire. It does not have anything to do with distance. There are two people in a relationship, and so there must always be mutuality in the relationship.

Low/Missing acknowledgement from partner. One of the first fundamental things that you need to do right now is to pull back your commitment. If you are not reciprocating a certain level of commitment from your partner, pull back. People are often of the belief that being in a long-distance relationship means low commitment. They tend to believe it is easy to play one person against the next just because they figure there is no way that either one of them will ever find out. As such, they play light with their commitment to the relationships while receiving full devotions from their partners.

If you have not been receiving the same level of commitment from your long-distance partner, you must learn to adjust your commitment to the relationship. If your partner cares, they will notice and will want to do something about it but be ready for the likelihood that they may not act at all. If your partner does not desire to commit to your long-distance relationship, they will not react when you pull back. Instead, they will remain on the same course or may even turn around and blame you for the lack of overall commitment in the relationship. You must keep your eyes open to this and do not hesitate to accept it. As much as it may hurt you to let go of love in the present moment, it will be one million times harder if you try to make it last longer than it should.

Clear your social media. Another thing that you will want to do is to clear clutter from any social media pages that you own. Let your social media page be a wonder to your non-acknowledging partner. If your partner does not acknowledge you on social media, save yourself some embarrassment by maintaining a conservative attitude towards the relationship as well. If you have posted, slowly begin to remove those post, bit by bit. Start by removing one post per day, that way you are gradually pulling back your acknowledgment without alerting many people and the best part, your partner will notice that you are doing it.

While you are doing all of this, keep in mind what the actual reason behind it is – to send a message to your partner. It is not every time that we are aware of what we do or of how what we do affect the people who we love. Look at this as a way to connect with your partner. If your partner cares about the acknowledgment of your relationship, they will confront you. If they confront you, use this opportunity to remind them about how you have felt about the missing acknowledgment to their friends and family on social media. When your partner explains their reason, if you understand the logic, proceed to a mutual resolution. There should be few problems in moving forward.

There is always more to learn about your partner in a long-distance relationship and so whenever you have these highly informative discussions, take what you learn and apply it immediately. Do not rush back into the way things were before you had the discussion. We all tend to do this sometimes, without the knowledge that we are doing it. Whenever we resolve an issue in our relationship, we tend to go back to doing the same things that we did before the discussion. Once you fix a problem in your relationship, take note of the changes. If your partner takes responsibility for not acknowledging you publicly, do not make any quick decisions. Wait and observe for changes in their behavior. Do not continue to do the same actions that you did before the discussion, as it would have effectively been a waste of precious time.

Your relationship must remain a mutual journey. Both you and your partner must put in the same amount of effort into building a relationship. It is easy to keep everything in your life separate from each other in a long-distance relationship, but you must strictly resist the temptation of being content with this. Your relationship must always maintain an open and honest atmosphere that invites you and your spouse into each other's lives. Nothing should be a secret or a mystery in your long-distance relationship. There is absolutely no space for additional complexities in your relationship. Neither you nor your partner should create barriers in your relationship that keeps each other at a distance. Always maintain an accommodating demeanor in your relationship.

– Financial openness –

Financial openness is usually a major point of anxiety for married couples, but because of the design of long-distance relationships, it is critical that you have no doubts about each other's finances from the initial stages of the relationship. It should not be a mystery. You should never hide or become scarce on the topic of money and finances in your long-distance relationship, neither should you have to guess or question the financial status of your partner. This information must be open and willingly shared in your relationship. If you find it difficult to approach your partner about finances, now is the perfect opportunity to talk to them about it. Do not allow your relationship to advance to a proposal and marriage with issues lingering around managing finances.

– Ill-intention –

If you are in a long-distance relationship or will be entering one, make every effort to protect yourself from ill-intent. Many people date long-distance with various ill-intentions. The most common amongst these is to obtain immigration status and financial support. It is fraud, and you must do everything in your power to protect yourself. It can be hard to tell if a partner is committing fraud since you invest emotionally in the relationship. You must make every effort to remain conscious of this factor. Do this by ensuring that your relationship always has balance. Everything that happens in your relationship must be by mutual effort. No partner should do more than the other, and no partner should contribute more than the other.

Fraud is a widespread problem in long-distance dating and the reason many people do not entertain the idea of a long-distance relationship. Always remain aware of the things that take place in your relationship. If you become confused or suspicious about some of your partner's actions, seek advice from someone who has appropriate experience in dealing with relationship issues. This person is usually the family pastor or a family therapist.

– Having the conversation on making the transition –

This conversation should not be too hard, and if it is, it may be because of some reservations by either you or your spouse. If your spouse solicits the reservation, do not jump to conclusions. I firmly believe that you should give your partner the benefit of the doubt, at least one time. Therefore, if the reservations are coming from your spouse, take it with a light heart and address the matter calmly. Your spouse may have a legitimate reason for opposing, and it is your responsibility to confirm this. Use your spouse's history of past behaviors to evaluate this matter. Has your spouse routinely objected to the idea of living together?

Some people have long-distance relationships for precise reasons. Some do it deliberately to keep their significant other a bay, and that works well for them. It does not mean that they are cheating or living a double life – it just means it is what is comfortable for them.

Therefore, it is imperative to find the exact cause of your spouse's reservations if they are having some. On the other side of giving the benefit of the doubt, there is always the chance that they do have ill-intentions. In this case, their intentions are only to get the benefits from the relationship, whether financial or otherwise, without making any further commitment. If this is the case, you will know it - trust me; more importantly, trust your gut.

14
– FINAL THOUGHTS –

Be careful about crossing boundaries in your relationship. Be mindful of the things that you say and the lines that you pass. Things always change in a long-distance relationship; some of those changes we advocate for, while others come as a side effect to the behaviors we portray in our relationships. Do not try to change any aspects of your long-distance relationship forcibly. More importantly, do not try to force your partner to adjust for any reason.

If your partner has qualities that you do not like or things that you believe that they can work on, speak with them calmly about it. Do not aggressively approach them or demand any immediate action from them. Let your partner know how you feel and then allow them enough time to process the information and to make the necessary changes.

In a previous relationship, I crossed a boundary that sent my relationship onto another path. After an argument that accompanied a tremendous disagreement, I decided to block my partner from being able to communicate with me. I knew my partner would try to smooth things over before the end of the day and I wanted to make sure that he could not do so. We had never done anything of the sort in our relationship, and I specifically remember us having a conversation about never doing such a thing to each other. Even though I remembered this promise, I wanted to be dramatic at the moment, and so I blocked my partner out of anger. I introduced "blocking" into the relationship. This one action that I took changed everything in the relationship. My partner was shocked and disappointed. It affected him more than I ever thought it would. The next thing you know, his first line of defense in every argument after that was to block me from his phone and social media pages. In hindsight, I think this may have been the moment that the relationship ended; even though it went on for years after that.

If something like this happens in your relationship, do not blame yourself. I take responsibility for my actions and realize that I did this action first; however, my partner is a mature individual who knew better and could have done better. This experience is one of those lightbulb moments in life that you do not forget. What you say and do in your long-distance relationship is what determines the faith of your relationship.

Ensure that you speak positivity into your relationship always. Resist the urge to get angry or to say things out of anger. Thoughts overflow and a lot of rushed decisions transpire when couples get mad. It becomes even worse if the line of communication gets interrupted or cut off. It sparks more anger and pushes people to make irrational decisions to seek attention. You can never know how your partner will receive the information that you send out to them. Be careful in what you say and do in your long-distance relationship. If what you have to say to your partner will not build, support, or grow your relationship, it is not that important to either your partner or to your relationship.

– Final advice on LDRs –

Do not freak out if as the days go by you find more things to not like about your partner. It is the spirit of fear, and it comes in many different forms. No one can ever love or like everything about their partner. It is just not possible. As you continue to talk to each other, there will be plenty of personality traits that you will notice and may not like. Gather everything that you learn about your partner over a period and form an idea of who your partner is. Try not to judge them based on one lousy incident or by one bad trait. It is entirely possible that they just had a stressful day on that specific day.

Do not judge your partner too soon either. Do not

take one extraordinary thing that they do once or now and then and glorify it. Wait, and follow their actions over a period. Allow them to prove themselves by showing consistency. Be patience and allow this process. Do not be too overly excited to fall in love. It will clutter your mind and cloud your judgment. In a long-distance relationship, you need to be able to think critically about matters concerning your relationship.

Remember that change is the only constant thing in our lives. We do not know what is going to happen or when it is going to happen. If you keep this in mind when you think about your relationship, you will begin to have a more open mind towards your partner when unexpected things happen. Learn to separate the things that have changed for good, from the ones that have changed for the worse. Knowing the difference between these changes when they happen, is the key to understanding what your next move will be in your relationship.

A long-distance relationship is a high maintenance relationship that includes a lot of talking and discussions, arguments and disagreements, understandings, misunderstandings, and re-understandings. It is an ongoing process of negotiating the best alternatives, based on the amount of change that is happening within the relationship.

When you are in a long-distance relationship, you are managing three lives; yours, your partner, and both of you together. That means you are actively conceptualizing three lives and executing the changes that happen daily in all three lives. I would say that is a significant accomplishment. Don't you think? If you are willing to look at the bigger picture, analyze the level of change that occurs in your relationship. Take the time out to evaluate these changes. Are they good or bad? What do you plan to do either way?

It may sound insane to you, but feelings do frequently change within the same relationship over a period. These feelings can change by the year, by the month, or even within the same day. It is how we grow in love. If things do not change and if feelings do not fluctuate, we would not be able to grow in love. This growth is what drives us to want to marry the person we claim to love. It is the abundance of the feeling of love that grows inside of us, that forces us to want to express more love.

The same goes for dislike or hate. Feelings do not only change for good; they change for the worst as well. It is okay to have shifts and changes in your feeling towards your partner. If they are more frequent than you believe to be normal, it is in your best interest to evaluate these feelings. These feelings could be internal, or they can also be from outside influencers. In any case, you must determine these feelings before advancing in your relationship.

The fear of making the wrong decision or of wasting your time can also have a substantial influence on your thought process in your long-distance relationship. Breathe. Take your relationship step by step. Yes, the loneliness is gruesome, and the heartache is unbearable, but you must learn to take it one day at a time. Do not dwell on insignificant things of little or no substance. Stay focus on the bigger picture – the future. Firmly reassure each other of your devotion daily.

When frustration settles in on your heart over matters of your long-distance relationship, create a distraction by investing significantly in the things that you have going on in your life. When things such as the need for sexual intercourse settles in on your body and your mind, distract your mind with the immediate and urgent things in your life. Something as simple as returning a phone call or running outside to your car or the mailbox creates the perfect distraction in situations like these. It will take some practice, but once you find what works best for you stick with it and perfect it.

Build a coping system. A coping system is a series of things that you say or do in different situations to offset the lack from your long-distance relationship. Build an internal system for sexual frustration, stress, loneliness, and all the other feelings that you experience in your relationship. These coping methods will transport you through the ordeal. If it does not work the first time, continue to work at it until you find something reliable that works for you.

– NOTE FROM AUTHOR –

I am blessed to have experienced some of the deepest and purest love long distance. If you feel that you have found love at a distance, take the chance at happiness. Do not let skeptics or fear deter you from your desires. I have lived some of the happiest times of my life dating long distance. I have also had some of the biggest mistakes of my life, and the most significant lessons of my life, dating long distance. Learn to trust yourself and to trust your instincts.

Long distance love is as real as any other love. The rush that you feel in always desiring your partner is next to Godliness. It is the purest feeling of love and affection. You will ignite in ways that you could have never imagined. Your thought process will develop, and your brain will learn how to create innovative ideas and principles that you will teach yourself.

There are millions of people across the globe in long-distance relationships. Therefore, there must be something about a long-distance relationship that is significantly benefiting that so many people risk so much to have it. As many people would not be in a long-distance relationship if there were no coping methods that work. They would not torture themselves on a day to day basis if their relationship did not fill them with hope and inspiration for the future. The discomfort and loneliness of a long-distance relationship would not be worth it if the joy of being with the one you love were not life-changing.

Long distance relationships are beautiful, and it is much manageable in these modern times to satisfy your need for your partner. Long distance relationships now have a conducive environment that nurtures growth, and so the possibility of building a future with your partner is possible if you follow the right steps. If you read this book to this point, I encourage you to apply all the principles and tools that I teach in this book. Make notes and highlight the sections that speak to your situation the most. Come back and reread those sections now and then to remind yourself of the steps that you need to take to move your long-distance relationship to the next phase. Keep firm in your beliefs and remember to always remain in control of the things that you allow to happen in your life. Good luck on your journey. I wish you all the best.